the
sewing machine
classroom

Learning the ins and outs of your machine

CHARLENE PHILLIPS

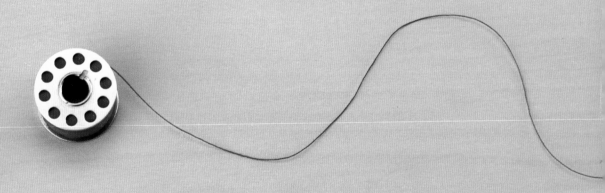

KRAUSE PUBLICATIONS
Cincinnati, Ohio

D1120171

The Sewing Machine Classroom Copyright © 2011 by Charlene Phillips. Manufactured in China. All rights reserved. No part of this book may be reproduced in any form or by any electronic or mechanical means including information storage and retrieval systems without permission in writing from the publisher, except by a reviewer who may quote brief passages in a review. Published by Krause Publications, a division of F+W Media, Inc., 10150 Carver Rd, Blue Ash, Ohio, 45242. (800) 289-0963. First Edition.

15 14 13 12 11   5 4 3 2 1

DISTRIBUTED IN CANADA BY FRASER DIRECT
100 Armstrong Avenue
Georgetown, ON, Canada L7G 5S4
Tel: (905) 877-4411

DISTRIBUTED IN THE U.K. AND EUROPE BY F&W MEDIA INTERNATIONAL
Brunel House, Newton Abbot, Devon, TQ12 4PU, England
Tel: (+44) 1626 323200, Fax: (+44) 1626 323319
Email: enquiries@fwmedia.com

DISTRIBUTED IN AUSTRALIA BY CAPRICORN LINK
P.O. Box 704, S. Windsor NSW, 2756 Australia
Tel: (02) 4577-3555

ISBN 13: 978-1-4402-1600-8
SRN: Y2994

Editor: Kelly Biscopink
Designer: Julie Barnett
Production coordinator: Greg Nock
Photographers: Ric Deliantoni and Christine Polomsky
Photo Stylist: Jen Wilson

www.fwmedia.com

metric conversion chart

to convert	to	multiply by
inches	centimeters	2.54
centimeters	inches	0.4
feet	centimeters	30.5
centimeters	feet	0.03
yards	meters	0.9
meters	yards	1.1

Measurements have been given in imperial inches with metric conversions in brackets—use one or the other as they are not interchangeable. The most accurate results will be obtained using inches.

ABOUT THE AUTHOR

Charlene Phillips is an author, magazine contributor, presenter and trainer. She lives in southwestern Ohio with her husband, Bryan. Together they own and operate The Sew Box, a store specializing in sewing machine feet, notions and self-designed sewing patterns. Since her mother taught her to sew at a very young age, Charlene has continued to learn and share sewing techniques with others, reaching "new sewing friends" around the world. More information can be found at www.thesewbox.com. Charlene enjoys hearing from others, and sharing tips through her blog at http://thesewbox.blogspot.com and www.sewingattachments.com. Continual sewing conversation can be found by joining her on facebook.com (The Sew Box).

Previously, Charlene owned an alterations business, was a school teacher, a college professor and an educational trainer for local schools. She is the author of *The Sewing Machine Attachment Handbook* and contributes to many magazines and online sites such as *Threads, Sew News, Creative Machine Embroidery* and *ISMACS News*. She is also a guest blogger for BERNINA Blog (www.berninausablog.com).

Charlene has presented and taught locally, as well as at various Quilt Markets and conferences.

DEDICATION

For my treasured grandchildren—Chance, Corin, Maggie and Robert—who always keep things in the right perspective.

ACKNOWLEDGMENTS

The questions, support and encouragement from many sewing friends around the world gave life and purpose to this book. Crafters are quick to share ideas, always having a zeal to learn new techniques. I wish to thank each and every one of you as we continue our learning journey together. I love your questions, comments and photos!

I wish to thank my husband, Bryan, for his encouragement and support during the many hours spent writing and sewing. Living in a house with a dedicated sewer requires tremendous patience and understanding of why every new notion and gadget is truly *needed*. Thank you Shirley, my beautiful daughter, for being my continual example of doing what you truly believe in. Thank you to my sons, Troy and Charles, for helping with all the computer and techie questions—from safely backing up the manuscript to keeping the music streaming from my iPod. Many thanks to their wonderful wives, Carrie and Tracy, for being there whenever needed.

Throughout my life, I have been blessed to be surrounded by a loving and supportive family who instilled the desire to learn and share with others. Thanks to my father, Charles Smith, my mother, Virgia Smith, and my stepmother, Dolores Smith, for never-ending love. Thanks to big brother, Mike Smith, for always being at the other end of the phone when I needed to talk, and to my sister, Monica Helton, who has always shown me how to never give up, no matter the odds.

This would only be words on paper without the fantastic and exciting crew at F+W Media. Editor Kelly Biscopink worked her magic to produce a concise and readable book from my scribblings, and the outstanding step-by-step photos are the talented work of Christine Polomsky. You are seeing the results of their true talent, while I enjoyed every fun minute spent with them. And the cheese cake! Thank you to Christine Doyle, Acquisitions Editor, for surrounding me with talent beyond words!

Thank you to both BERNINA of America, Inc. and the Singer Sewing Machine Company for the fabulously wonderful loaner sewing machines used for the photo shoot and throughout the writing, sewing and editing of the book.

And to you, the reader—I hope you enjoy the collaborative efforts of the very talented and supportive people in my life.

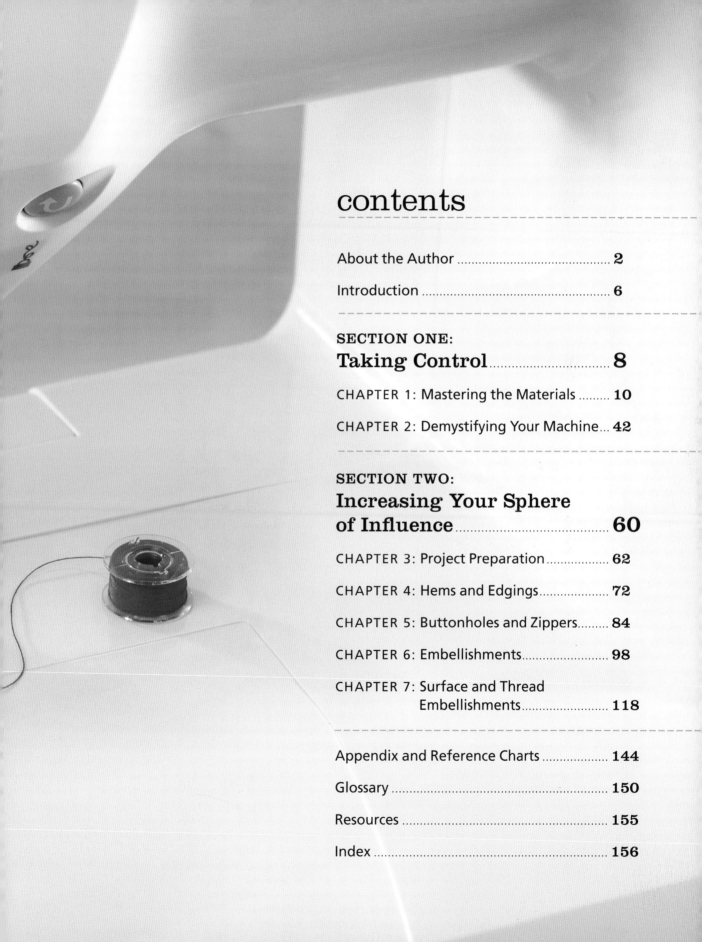

contents

introduction

All of us start at the same place—the beginning. Over the years I have had my share of puckered seams, creeping fabric, tangled threads and tunneled stitching. Although some days I still find my trash can more full of trials-and-errors than my finished pile, I eventually know what is going wrong...once I stop to analyze and think about it! Experimenting with fabrics, needles, threads and stabilizers, and learning what my sewing machine can do *for* me has resulted in more enjoyable sewing time and less frustration. Whether piecing quilts or sewing up a new wardrobe, I would rather spend my time sewing than grabbing the seam ripper!

Every sewer—new and experienced—encounters stitch problems from time to time, and knowing what to troubleshoot first can be extremely helpful. Diagnosing and remedying common problems ends frustration, keeps your creative juices flowing and gives you the confidence to try new techniques. You'll be able to sew up a beautiful wardrobe like a professional when you know the correct needle to use and how to use the gorgeous threads that are available.

To sew something you are proud of, it must be durable, have straight, even stitches, and look just as good after several washings as when it was first finished. For thousands of years, sewing was done by hand. With the invention of the sewing machine came timesaving techniques, but also the beginning of tangled threads and broken needles. It's time for *you* to take control!

Your machine may be capable of doing so much more than you realize. Learn all those timesaving features—they're right at your fingertips! Once you master your machine, there will be more time to enjoy trying new sewing techniques. There are many bits of sewing information in books, magazines and on the Internet. Looking through my own sewing journal, I have pulled out what was beneficial to me over the years to share with you. Hopefully, you will find a sewing nugget or two of information that you can add to your own journal.

Although it is tempting to learn a new technique while in the process of sewing up a new project, it is always better to pause and take time to learn and perfect that same technique through simple practice. Learn it, and then continue to add to your repertoire by changing fabrics, needles, threads or sewing feet. Make the technique yours, and then use it on your next sewing project for perfect results.

It's time to reach into your fabric stash, grab some needles and thread and begin sewing!

taking control

Control those things that affect all your stitching! Puckered fabric and uneven stitches are not what you want when sewing a special project. With most stitch problems, our first instinct is to blame the sewing machine's tension, but the guilty culprit can be an incorrect needle, faulty thread, lack of fabric preparation or even a linty sewing machine.

Precision is important! Topstitching must be evenly spaced, blind hems must be invisible and zippers attractively stitched. Faulty stitching detracts from all your hard work, and you will end up hiding the end product instead of enjoying it.

Control the things you can to make a perfect stitch and a more perfect project!

mastering the materials

A visit to any fabric store surrounds you with luscious fabrics in all colors, types and textures—silks to be admired and furs to be touched! Sewing projects immediately form in your head as you wander aisle after aisle of fabric. As you grab a bolt and head to the cutting counter, pause and read the end of the bolt. What's the fabric made of? Is it a silky blend? What special threads, needles or stabilizers are needed to sew a perfect project? Understanding your materials will help ensure a beautiful finished project!

THE PERFECT STITCH

Thread passes through the needle eye in an up-and-down motion very quickly before it forms one stitch. The threaded needle pierces the fabric and enters the bobbin area where a hook catches the upper thread. The hook carries the thread all around the bobbin case so it makes one wrap of the bobbin thread. The take-up lever pulls excess thread from the bobbin area and back to the top, forming a lockstitch. Ideally, a lockstitch falls in the middle of the fabric. The feed dogs pull the fabric along, and everything is repeated over and over again. Forming a perfect stitch begins with three things we normally don't think about: thread, needle and tension.

When beginning a sewing project, choosing the perfect fabric is usually what we think about first. With great care and enjoyment, we think about fabric type and colors to best suit our project. We may then choose thread based on a nice color match, and grab needles just in case those at home break. Admittedly, thread and needle choice is not as exciting as choosing fabric, but they may be the most important items we choose.

Learn to know your thread. For the best results, always choose high-quality thread which is smooth and doesn't split easily. Lower-quality thread has frayed edges and roughness which create excessive lint buildup and a multitude of stitching problems.

After choosing fabric to suit your project:

• Choose thread that's compatible with the fabric type and weight.
• Select the proper needle type that is compatible with your fabric.
• Select a needle size to match the thread.

sewing 101

Is it hard to thread the needle? The needle size may be too small for the thread. Refer to the chart on page 145 for choosing the perfect needle and thread combo for any project.

KEEP A JOURNAL

Each new combination of stitches, fabric or threads can result in machine adjustments. Keep a sewing journal of stitch samples and machine settings for future reference. Reach into your fabric scrap basket and start sewing. Whether learning new techniques or using a new sewing foot, jot down notes as you go. Did you increase or decrease tension for certain fabrics? Did stitch patterns change when increasing stitch width? How did you keep two thread colors from tangling with twin needles? Sew out some stitch samples to place with your notes. No journal? Try index cards!

Keep a sewing journal with notes on your sewing experiments!

the importance of thread

Although economically enticing to use one spool of thread for all your projects, whether silk, vinyl, crepe or cottons...think twice! A spool of cotton/polyester thread may not produce perfect results on silky or stretchy fabrics. Choosing the proper thread is crucial to eliminating frustration later.

THREAD QUALITY

Years ago, I always bought thread on sale. The cheaper the better—five spools for a dollar was always so enticing. Why not buy a lot and store it until needed? Had I given a thought to thread quality, I could have saved myself many problematic issues of thread breakage, weak seams, skipped stitches and balled up tangles of thread. Add excessive lint buildup and trouble was inevitable.

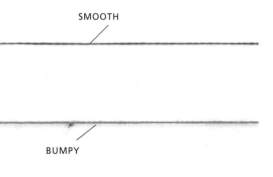

SMOOTH

BUMPY

Choose a good quality thread for your sewing projects to achieve maximum results.

We have so many thread choices with the many quality threads on the market today. They may initially cost more, but quality thread can help eliminate many sewing frustrations. Try several brands with your sewing machine and see which behaves best. Your machine may have a preference.

To form a stitch, thread passes through tension discs, thread guides and through the needle—up and down the threading path and into the bobbin area, catching the bobbin thread perfectly. There are many chances of breakage as thread travels along this path. Continual lint buildup and pieces of thread caught in the tension discs ultimately create problems with maintaining a balanced tension.

Magnify different threads, and you will clearly see the difference between those with fraying fibers and those with a smooth finish. Hold a piece up to the light and notice any fuzzy or loose threads. Poor quality thread is also twisted unevenly, having thick and thin areas. Toss it!

So which thread to use? Higher quality cotton threads can be labeled mercerized, extra long staple, Egyptian or Peruvian. Although it is not as durable, strong or elastic as polyester, choose cotton thread when sewing natural fiber fabrics like silk, cotton, wool and linen. Choose synthetic polyester when sewing leather, vinyls, imitation leather and suede. Silk thread is a good choice when basting or sewing sheer fabrics as the thread is nearly invisible, and the fineness creates less bulk in the seams.

HOW THREAD IS MADE

We can place thread into four categories based on the material used:

- Natural fiber is made from animal (wool, silk) and plant (cotton, flax, jute).
- Rayon fiber is made from cellulose.
- Man-made fiber is made from mineral (glass, metallic).
- Synthetic fiber is made from polyester, nylon, elastic, acrylic or polypropylene.

Threads begin as simple yarns. Twisting short fibers or continuous filaments produces these yarns and is responsible for the flexibility and strength of a good sewing thread. Two or more yarns are combined in this way, and then a *reverse twist* is added to make thread. Without the reverse twist, threads would separate when passing through the needle and tension discs.

Twists are the number of turns per inch put in the thread. Too little twist results in thread that frays and breaks. Too much twist results in thread that snarls, loops and knots. For machine sewing, an additional left twist (Z twist) may be added. The action of sewing will increase the left twisted thread, so if the thread was twisted entirely to the right, it would become untwisted. To test the twist, hold the spool in your left hand, and roll the strand of thread towards you with one thumb. Left twist will tighten and right twist will loosen.

Ply is the number of yarns twisted together to make a thread. Two-ply thread is two yarns twisted together and three-ply is three yarns twisted.

Thread finishes are added for varying sewing uses. *Soft* thread is left unfinished and only dyed and lubricated. *Mercerized* thread is cotton thread treated in a caustic solution that allows the fibers to swell and take dye more readily, while also increasing strength and luster. *Gassed* thread is mercerized cotton that is passed quickly through a flame to reduce fuzz, resulting in a higher sheen and a soft, iridescent appearance. *Glazed* thread is cotton thread that is treated with starches and other chemicals, heated, and polished for high luster.

THREAD WEIGHT

Sewing machine thread comes in weights from very fine to heavyweight. The most commonly used thread is all-purpose, medium-weight thread.

Here are a few tips on choosing a thread weight:

- For general sewing, buttonholes and topstitching on medium-weight fabrics, use all-purpose or regular threads.
- For general sewing, buttonholes and topstitching on delicate, lightweight fabrics, use extra-fine cotton-covered polyester, fine cotton machine embroidery, lightweight polyester or lightweight silk thread.
- For general sewing, buttonholes and topstitching on heavyweight fabrics, use topstitching, machine embroidery or heavy threads.
- The heavier the fabric, the heavier the thread weight.

Experiment with different thread weights to find what suits your sewing project for elasticity, strength, durability and appearance. Using a thread that's too thin for topstitching will mar your garment's appearance. Read the thread spool! You will generally find information to guide thread selection: manufacturer, color number, fiber content, weight and number of plys, and whether or not the thread is mercerized.

 sewing 101

If your machine has a vertical thread spool, place the thread on your machine with the top part of the spool up. How can you tell top from bottom? When placed on the spool pin, the thread should unwind from behind the thread spool. Always check each thread spool for burrs that can cause the thread to catch and break.

THREAD TYPES

All-Purpose Thread

All-purpose thread is usually made from cotton-wrapped polyester. Cotton gives the thread strength, and polyester gives it flexibility and stretch. All-purpose thread can be used on many fabric types, especially blends. For heavyweight fabrics, use 40 weight thread. The cotton thread fibers have been mercerized to add strength, ability to take dye and add color fastness.

100 Percent Polyester

Polyester thread provides strength and flexibility when sewing knits and stretchy fabrics as the thread stretches and doesn't shrink. It is perfect on natural fabrics, fabrics with blended fibers and synthetic fabrics. Polyester thread sews well at high speeds with less breakage. It has more stitch volume and works well for satin stitches. It's also more "forgiving" of mechanical conditions of the machine or poor adjustments. Wind the bobbin slowly—polyester thread has some stretch to it; if the thread stretches, the seams will pucker.

100 Percent Cotton

Cotton thread is made from a yarn of plant origin, such as cotton or linen. One hundred percent cotton thread is best for use on cotton and linen fabrics.

100 Percent Mercerized Cotton

Mercerized cotton thread is treated with a caustic solution which causes fibers to swell and increases luster and strength. Because it's preshrunk, it tends not to shrink like regular cotton thread.

Silk

Silk thread is strong and has a bit of stretch; it is smooth and free of "fuzzies." Silk thread blends almost invisibly into seams. It is perfect for basting as it doesn't leave an impression on the fabric. Silk thread takes on the color of the fabric, so a huge color assortment is unnecessary. Perfect for sewing all fabrics, it is excellent for sewing silks and woolens. Silk thread also does a beautiful job sewing rolled hems with a tighter edge.

(continued on page 16...)

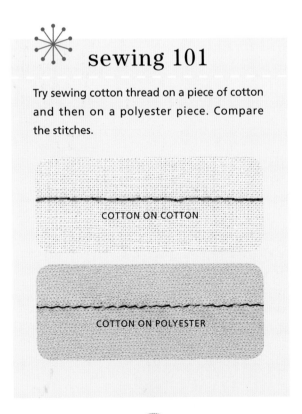

sewing 101

Try sewing cotton thread on a piece of cotton and then on a polyester piece. Compare the stitches.

COTTON ON COTTON

COTTON ON POLYESTER

RIBBON FLOSS

BUTTON AND CARPET

LINGERIE

JEANS

METALLIC (MEDIUM WEIGHT)

SILVER METALLIC

METALLIC (VISCOSE
AND METALLIS)

SILK RIBBON

PEARL CROWN RAYON

(Thread Types continued...)

Nylon

Nylon thread is heavy duty, abrasion resistant and doesn't deteriorate. It is perfect for both indoor and outdoor projects, and is available in many colors. Use nylon thread for upholstery and heavy-duty home decorating projects. Nylon thread can melt at low iron temperatures. Choose a needle size to match the thread weight.

Fusible

Fusible thread provides a temporary bond until final stitching. It melts together when pressed with a steam iron. Use it on hard-to-sew fabrics, such as suedes, knits and leathers. Fusible thread keeps both fabrics in place during permanent stitching, preventing creeping.

Rayon

Rayon thread has a smooth finish, a pronounced sheen, and provides consistent, trouble-free sewing. Oftentimes used for machine embroidery, it holds up to high-speed sewing without fraying. Use it for decorative stitching, such as embroidery, thread art, satin stitching and couching. Rayon thread comes in an array of colors, and is generally available in 30 and 40 weights.

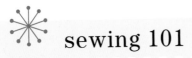

sewing 101

Keeping rayon and metallic thread in the freezer prolongs its lifespan!

Metallic

Metallic thread is available from fine to heavyweight. The finer thread is used for machine sewing, and thicker threads can be couched or used for bobbin work. Always use a metallic needle and sew at a slower speed to prevent thread breakage. There are various types of metallic threads, such as silver metallic and those made of viscose/metallis blends. It is available in variety of textures and thicknesses from 12 weight to 50 weight. The finer 50 weight is perfect for fine monograms, filigree embroidery and intricate stitching. Use needle size 100/16 when sewing with 20 weight, and use a 120/19 wing needle if hemstitching.

Monofilament (Invisible)

Monofilament thread is made of 100% transparent nylon or polyester, and is available in clear and smoke. Use in the bobbin when bobbin thread shouldn't show or use as upper thread when couching (see pages 124–125) shouldn't detract from the underlying threads. This thread is strong with a little stretch. The most popular sizes are .004 and .005. Use for appliqué, sewing crafts, machine quilting and home decor projects. Cover the spool with a spool net when machine sewing to prevent tangling.

Pearl Cotton

Pearl cotton thread can be cotton or rayon. It is available in three weights—5, 8 and 12. A 2-ply, high-sheen, non-divisible twisted pearl cotton thread (one strand) is used in many forms of needlework. It is oftentimes used in the bobbin area only for bobbin work or decorative stitches. When used for couching (see pages 124–125), couch over two or more threads.

Jeans

Jeans thread is heavyweight and makes a durable stitch. Use it for machine embroidery, topstitching and general sewing of denims. Colors Blue Jean Gold and Indigo match traditional blue jean colors. Use it with a jeans/denim needle.

sewing 101

Does your thread tend to twist and knot during hand sewing? The proper method is to thread the needle with the tail that comes off the spool. Thread does have a "nap," so instead of folding the thread over and knotting it, cut a second piece of thread and thread both ends in the needle eye. Your thread is now doubled, but not twisted.

Silk Ribbon

Silk ribbon is a flat, lightweight ribbon that is soft and pliable. Sizes 2mm and 4mm can be used for couching, embroidery or bobbin work. Wind it onto a bobbin by hand or very slowly by machine. Use a heavy tapestry needle to pull the ribbon to the wrong side of the fabric at the beginning and ending of stitching to tie off.

Ribbon Floss

Ribbon floss is small, thin ribbon that is braided, not woven; it has great pliability and reduced twisting. It is usually rayon, but metallic ribbon floss is also available. Use ribbon floss for bobbin work and hand embroidery. When used in the bobbin, wind it by hand or very slowly by machine.

Silk Buttonhole Twist

Typically used for hand sewing buttonholes, this thread can also be used for silk ribbon embroidery, bobbin work or crazy quilt embellishments. It is available in sizes 6, 8, 10 and 12. Size 6 is heaviest, and size 10 is the most common. When hand sewing, thread the loose end of the thread onto the needle and knot the end that was closest to the spool.

Basting

Basting thread is a soft, cotton thread that breaks easily. Use it for basting seams and tailor's tacks.

Bobbin

Bobbin thread is a fine 60 or 70 weight thread made from cotton and polyester. It is typically used for embroidery, but can be used for many sewing techniques. It is available in black or white. Although not as strong as regular thread, it can be used in the bobbin for piecing a quilt or general sewing. Its fine, thin quality results in a flatter and more accurate seam allowance.

Water-Soluble Basting

Water-soluble basting thread provides a temporary hold until final stitching. It dissolves when steam pressed or washed. It can be used used in the bobbin and the needle.

Lingerie

Lingerie thread is an extra-fine nylon thread with some stretch. It is available in black and white. Use it for sewing tricot, lingerie and lightweight woven synthetics. It can be used in the bobbin for free-motion sewing or embroidery.

Button and Carpet

This is a cotton-wrapped polyester, strong, heavyweight thread. Use it for sewing buttons and heavy-duty items.

CHOOSING AND
CARING FOR THREAD

- Numbers on thread spools (i.e. 40/3, 100/3) need not be confusing. The first number is the size of the thread. The second number is the number of plys of the thread when twisted together; the more plys, the stronger the thread. A general rule is to use two ply for decorative stitching and three ply for general purpose stitching. Remember, thread quality and strength has evolved over the years, so try many brands.

- The higher the number, the finer the thread. The medium size is 40–50 weight. Thread sizes range up to 100.

- Thread weight is not always listed on the spool, as cotton and polyester threads are sized and coded differently. For example, all-purpose cotton thread 50/3 and polyester 100/3 have differing numbers but are similar in size.

- When selecting silk thread, 100 weight is best as it is the smallest size available and can be used with any fabric. Silk is also available in 30 and 50 weight.

- When letters indicate size, A is fine and D is heavy.

- What color to use? Select one shade darker than the fabric. If fabric is multicolored or plaid, choose the most dominant color.

- Thread deteriorates over time. Store it away from extreme moisture or dryness in a covered container to keep the thread free from dust. Toss out (and don't look back!) thread that is extremely old or hasn't been cared for properly.

Look at the end or side of your thread spool for important information about that specific thread.

PROPER THREAD PLACEMENT

How the thread spool is placed on the sewing machine is usually overlooked as a culprit of stitch problems, yet a few things are important to note. Take a quick look at the thread on your machine. How does it unwind? Around the front or back of the spool? What is the shape of the thread spool? Although seemingly minor, proper spool placement is important to the thread's delivery to the needle.

- If the spool is a typical spool (symmetrical at both ends), it is meant to unwind from the side, not the top. Place the thread on the vertical spool pin and thread the machine as normal. Place the thread spool so it unwinds from the back of the spool. If your machine came with a small felt pad, place it under the thread spool.

- If the spool is cone-shaped, it is cross-wound and meant to unroll from the top of the cone. Some newer machines have a second spool pin that lays horizontally, which is preferable for cone-shaped spools. However, if your machine has only a vertical spool pin and the cone-shaped spool doesn't sit properly on it, invest in a thread stand. Place the stand behind the machine, put the spool on it, and thread normally.

- Whether vertical or horizontal placement, be sure to use a spool cap that matches the end size of the thread spool. Have you ever had the thread become a tangled mess wrapped around the thread spool? Using a thread cap can eliminate this problem.

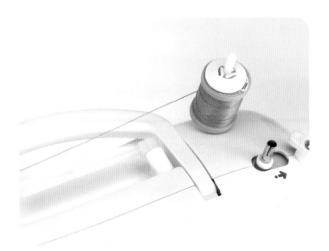

Place a typical thread spool vertically so it unwinds from the back of the spool.

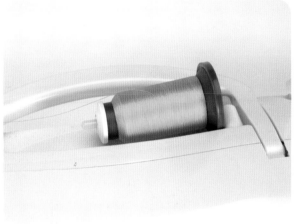

Place a cone-shaped spool horizontally so it unwinds from the top of the spool.

the perfect needle

Just as important as using a working sewing machine, using the correct needle is crucial. Broken threads, skipped stitches and other thread problems are usually the result of an improper or damaged needle. To avoid stitch problems, choose the best needle for the task.

PARTS OF A NEEDLE

- **Shank:** The shank is the part of the needle that is inserted into the sewing machine.

- **Shaft**: The shaft is the body of the needle, or how thick the needle is. A Microtex needle has a thin shaft, and a jeans needle has a heavy-duty shaft.

- **Front groove**: The front groove allows thread to lay flat and close to the needle as it goes down the needle to the bobbin. Some needles have a deeper groove which protects the thread from friction. If the needle is too fine or too large for the thread, improper stitches result.

- **Scarf:** The scarf is the indentation at the back of the needle, where the stitch is formed. As the bobbin shuttle swings into the scarf, it hooks into the looped needle thread to create the stitch.

- **Eye:** The eye is the hole where thread passes through the needle. The size of the eye varies by needle type. Select a needle size to appropriately fit the thread size.

- **Point:** Point type is the deciding factor when choosing a needle to match a fabric. A jeans needle will have a sharp point, whereas a jersey/ballpoint needle has a rounded point.

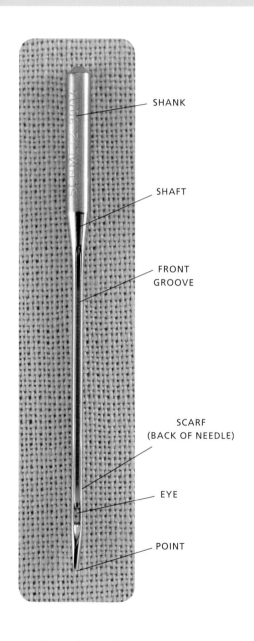

SHANK

SHAFT

FRONT GROOVE

SCARF (BACK OF NEEDLE)

EYE

POINT

Parts of a needle

NEEDLE BASICS

There are three things to consider when choosing a needle:

- Needle system

- Needle point or type

- Needle size

Remember that thread selection is very important, but just as important is matching the thread type and weight with the correct needle. The sewing machine needle is the least expensive sewing notion, so change it often!

An improper needle forces the thread through the fabric, instead of allowing it to flow smoothly through the needle hole and into the fabric. The needle eye must be large enough for thread to pass through easily to minimize friction. If the needle is hard to thread, the eye may be too small for the thread; try a larger size.

A common mistake is using a needle that is too small. A size 70 works best for delicate fabrics like chiffon, but if using a lighter thread such as lingerie thread, use a smaller size needle such as 60 or 65. Always start with the smaller needle (which makes a smaller hole in the fabric) and move to the next size if skipped stitching occurs. As a general rule, the needle eye should be about 40 percent larger than the thread diameter. For general sewing, try using needle size 75/11 or 80/12 for 40 weight thread, and 90/14 or 100/16 for 30 weight thread.

Thread should move smoothly down the groove on the front of the needle. Thin thread in a thick needle gives the thread too much "play," leading to skipped stitches and thread damage (fraying). Thick thread in a fine needle forces the thread to rub against the edges of the groove, leading to thread jams and breaks.

sewing 101

The long set of numbers on a needle packet is called the *needle system*. The most common needle system for household sewing machines is system 130/705 H. These needles are the same as 15x1 H needles (Japanese) and 2020 (Singer). The number 130 refers to the length of the shank and 705 means the backside is flat. Almost all household sewing machines require a needle with a flattened shank, but refer to your sewing machine owner's manual for specific instructions on the needle system required for your machine.

SIZES AND TYPES OF NEEDLES

Sewing machine needles range in size from 60/8 to 120/19. These numbers refer to the size of the needle shaft (the diameter of the needle at the needle eye). The first number is European/metric and the second is the U.S. sizing system.

Common sizes and appropriate fabrics:

- For most natural and synthetic fabrics: 60/8 to 100/16

- For jersey and stretch: 70/10 to 90/14

- For heavyweight and topstitching: 80/12 to 100/16

- For hemstitch (wing): 100/16 to 120/19

sewing 101

Change your needle after every six or eight hours of sewing. Synthetic fabrics tend to dull needles quickly. Remember, the average project can contain as many as 50,000 stitches or more!

UNDERSTANDING A NEEDLE PACKET

There is a lot of information on a needle packet. So what does it all mean? Use the photo at right as an example.

- **Needle type**: In the example, the needle type is Leather. LL and NTW also refer to the fact that this needle is a leather needle.

- **Needle system**: The needle system in the example is 130/705 HLL. H stands for Hohlkehle, which is German for "with scarf". The last letters are for type of needle (LL for leather). Refer to your sewing machine owner's manual for the type of needle system to use with your machine.

- **Needle size**: 90/14 refers to the diameter of the needle blade in hundredths of a millimeter measured above the scarf. 90 is this European measurement, 14 is the U.S. reference number.

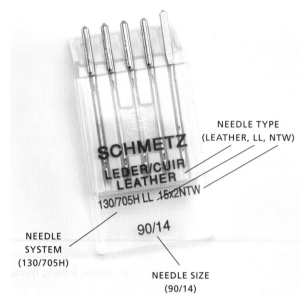

NEEDLE TYPE (LEATHER, LL, NTW)

NEEDLE SYSTEM (130/705H)

NEEDLE SIZE (90/14)

Understanding a needle packet

sewing 101: understanding needles

- There were many size designations for early needles. In 1953, metric size was designated. The abbreviation NM was introduced. If you see this abbreviation, NM stands for *number metric*.

- The European metric needle sizing system numbers from 60 to 120. The American needle sizing system numbers from 8 to 19. On a 90/14 needle packet, 90 is European sizing and 14 is American sizing.

- Remember, the lighter the fabric, the smaller the needle size; the heavier the fabric, the larger the needle size. The needle is then matched to thread size: the smaller the size of the needle, the smaller the eye hole and therefore, the finer the thread.

- The most common sewing machine needles used are 65/9, 75/11 and 80/12. Knowing the differences of each needle size prevents needle breakage, skipped stitches and other stitch problems.

- Size 65/9 is used when curves are sharp and stitches are dense, and for small detail work.

- Size 75/11 is used mainly with embroidery machines. This needle's diameter is the right size for embroidery and provides enough strength for the work.

- Size 80/12 is used for much of our general sewing and even some heavier fabrics, such as denim. The needle's diameter provides the necessary strength.

- Every time you change the needle size, you are actually changing the tension of the top thread and the way the needle penetrates the fabric.

UTILITY NEEDLES

Jeans/Denim

A jeans or denim needle has an extra large eye, a sharp point and a large groove to accommodate thick threads. Use one for sewing denim, densely woven fabrics, and to achieve a very straight stitch on layered fabrics. Sizes 70/10, 75/11, 80/12, 90/14, 100/16, 110/18. Available as twin needle size 4.0/100.

Jersey (Ballpoint)

This needle has a rounded tip that separates fibers instead of cutting them, eliminating damage to the fabric while sewing. Use one when sewing knits and stretch fabrics, artificial fur, knit cotton, gauze, jersey, lycra, sweatshirt, tulle and lingerie. Sizes 70/10, 75/11, 80/12, 90/14, 100/16, 110/18.

Leather

A leather needle has a slightly twisted, wedge-shaped point which pierces leather easier than a regular sewing machine needles. It cuts as it penetrates and reduces friction. Use one for sewing leather, artificial leather and heavy nonwoven fabrics. Sizes 70/10, 80/12, 90/14, 100/16, 110/18, 120/19.

Microtex

A microtex needle has a thin shaft and a sharp point. Use one for straight stitching on delicate and microfiber fabrics, artificial leather, brocade, chiffon, coated fabrics, crepe, foils, lamé, nylon, oil cloth, polyester and silk. This needle is fragile, so it should be changed frequently. Sizes 60/8, 65/9, 70/10, 75/11, 80/12, 90/14.

Stretch

A stretch needle has a rounded point and a deep scarf to help prevent skipped stitches. Use one when sewing jersey, knit cotton, lycra, lingerie, velour jersey, synthetic suede and elastic knitwear. Sizes 70/10, 75/11, 80/12, 90/14. Available as twin needle sizes 2.5/75, 3.0/75 (see page 24).

sewing 101

A stretch needle is better than a ballpoint or Jersey needle for sewing elastic. It has a medium ballpoint and a special eye and scarf.

Topstitch

A topstitch needle has an extra large eye, a sharp point and an enlarged groove for larger diameter threads. Sizes 80/12, 90/14, 100/16.

Universal

A universal needle has a slightly rounded, tapered point so it slips through knits without causing runs. Use one for general sewing, and with woven and knit fabrics. Sizes 60/8, 65/9, 70/10, 75/11, 80/12, 90/14, 100/16, 110/18, 120/19.

sewing 101

- Titanium needles are layered with titanium to last much longer. They are said to be stronger than regular needles.

- Teflon-coated machine needles help the needle slide through fabric more easily. Teflon needles are useful for waterproof fabrics with a special coating that may stick to the needle.

SPECIALTY NEEDLES

Specialty needles expand the versatility of your sewing machine while adding texture and embellishment. Choosing appropriate needles can minimize stitch problems while adding a personal flair to your project. With the correct combination of needle and thread, you will achieve perfect stitches. Remember, fabric type determines thread weight, needle size and needle type; correct needle size depends on the thread and fabric.

Embroidery

An embroidery needle is extremely sharp with an elongated eye to pierce the fabric and accomodate weaker embroidery thread. The distance between the eye and point decreases the chance of needle dragging on the fabric and resulting needle breaks. A fine needle size 8 or 9 is good for lightweight, sheer fabrics; middle-weight size 14 or 16 is used for most projects; heavyweight size 19 or 20 is used for heavyweight fabrics. Also available as twin needle.

Twin Embroidery

A twin embroidery needle has two embroidery needles on one shank. Use it for pin tucks, embroidery and topstitching.

Double Eye

A double eye needle has two eyes, one right over the other, allowing the use of two thread colors while stitching. Use two spools of thread with each unwinding in the opposite direction to prevent tangling. System 130/705 DE. Also available: triple eye: 2.5/80, 3.0/80.

Metallic

A metallic needle has an enlarged square eye and a large groove to prevent shredding and breaking of metallic threads. It is useful for topstitching, embroidery, quilting and decorative stitching. Sizes 70/10, 80/12, 90/14. Twin sizes 2.8/80, 3.0/90.

Quilting

Quilting needles are designed with a thin, tapered point to pass through multiple layers. Choose the size specific for piecing or quilting: sizes 75/11 (for piecing with

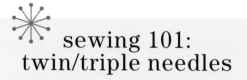

sewing 101: twin/triple needles

Two (or three) needles on one shaft create two (three) rows of stitches at the same time. Two (three) spools are used. Available in universal, stretch, jeans, metallic, embroidery and wing (hemstitch). They are perfect for pin tucks, topstitching and decorative stitching. Use twin needle size 2.0 for gathering. Twin sizes: 1.6/70, 1.6/80, 2.0/80, 2.5/80, 3.0/80, 3.0/90, 4.0/80, 4.0/90, 6.0/100, 8.0/100. (First number is width between needles, second number is needle size.) Use with a wide (zigzag) needle plate to avoid breakage.

50 weight thread), 80/12 and 90/14 (for piecing with 40 weight thread).

Spring

The needle is set inside a spring which prevents fabric from riding up on the needle, eliminating the need for a presser foot (remove presser foot when using). Use for freehand embroidery, quilting and monograms. Sizes 70/10, 80/12, 90/14.

Twin Stretch

This needle has two stretch needles combined on one shank. Use it for seams, hems, decorative stitching and topstitching on knits.

Wing (Hemstitch)

This needle has a very wide flange (wing) on the side; a sharp point makes holes in the fabric without cutting the fabric's threads. Use it with light- and medium-weight fabrics. Perfect for heirloom sewing, cutwork or creating holes for edged crochet. Sizes 100/16, 120/19. Twin size 100/16. Use with a wide (zigzag) needle plate.

Twin Wing (Hemstitch)

This needle has one universal needle and one flange (wing) needle for making one large hole and one small hole in the fabric. Use for decorative and open work stitching.

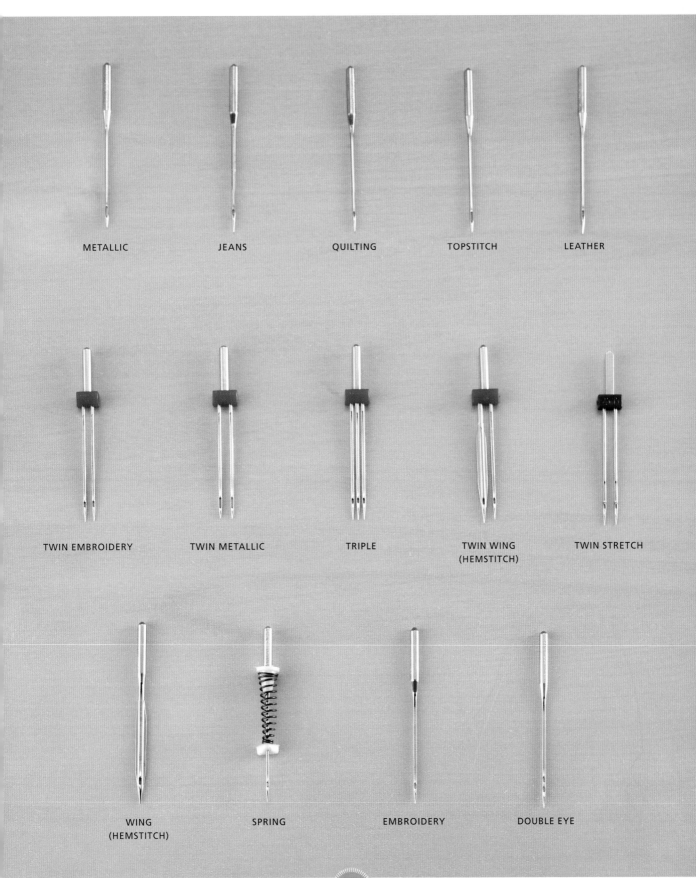

METALLIC

JEANS

QUILTING

TOPSTITCH

LEATHER

TWIN EMBROIDERY

TWIN METALLIC

TRIPLE

TWIN WING
(HEMSTITCH)

TWIN STRETCH

WING
(HEMSTITCH)

SPRING

EMBROIDERY

DOUBLE EYE

fabrics

There are hundreds of fabric types, and you will find that many are sewn with the same techniques. Choosing the correct fabric for your pattern shouldn't be hit-or-miss. Armed with some knowledge of fabric, you will have more top-of-the-line successes than failures. When in doubt, make fabric selections based on the pattern's suggestions. Have a lovely fabric that may be hard to sew? Choose an easy design that has minimal seams. Stitch out some test swatches and make notes for future reference.

GRAIN

Each piece of woven fabric has a crosswise and lengthwise grain. Pattern pieces are placed on the fabric according to the grain of the fabric. If the fabric is off-grain when the pattern piece is cut, the garment can be twisted and bias areas will not be the true bias. Ever had a pair of jeans twist after washing? The fabric wasn't cut on-grain.

A few terms are important to understanding grain of fabric:

- **The selvage** runs along the edge of the finished fabric. Usually this edge has the manufacturer's name on it, and oftentimes color-match dots. If you tug on the selvage, it doesn't give. The selvage must always be removed before cutting the fabric.

- **The lengthwise grain** (warp threads) runs parallel to the selvage. Hold the fabric in both hands along the lengthwise grain and tug—there is very little "stretch" in the fabric along the lengthwise grain.

- **The crosswise grain** (weft threads) runs perpendicular to the selvage. Hold the fabric in both hands along the crosswise grain and tug—there is more stretch in this direction.

- **The true bias** runs at a 45-degree angle to the selvage. Pulling on the true bias gives quite a lot of stretch.

Understanding fabric grain is important, especially when laying out pattern pieces. Clothes are designed to have very little stretch in some areas and more stretch in others. Proper placement of the pattern along the correct grain is crucial to achieving optimum results.

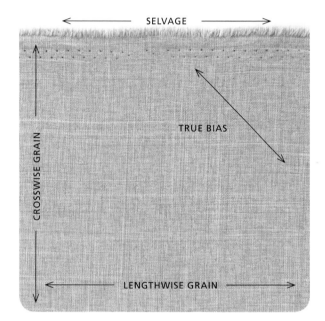

Knowing the grain of your fabric eliminates twisting later.

sewing 101

Warp threads are stretched on the loop and made secure. They become the lengthwise grain. Weft threads are woven back and forth, perpendicular to the warp threads. They become the crosswise grain. Selvages are the outer edges of the fabric and are made when the weft threads change direction.

KNOWING THE GRAIN

Woven fabrics can be off-grain when cut from the bolt if their lengthwise and crosswise grains are not perfectly perpendicular. Oftentimes, one side must be straightened. See page 64 for how to check and straighten the grain. Patterns are designed so the grain line marking is perfectly parallel to the selvage whether cut on the lengthwise grain or the bias. Follow the arrows! Accurate grain lines and accurate measures are crucial to having successful results.

FABRIC GRAIN TIPS:

- Inspect the fabric for creases that won't press out or other irregularities. Place pattern pieces away from those areas so that section of fabric isn't used.

- Lay the fabric on a flat surface—don't allow it to hang off a table. Many fabrics will stretch out of shape when hanging and can become distorted.

- Place all pattern pieces on the fabric so the top of each piece is going the same direction. This ensures that even the slightest difference in nap, print, weave or directional print is not noticeable when sewn.

- Don't place any pattern piece on the selvage.

- Pins can leave marks in delicate fabrics, so use weights instead.

- Silky and slippery fabrics shouldn't be folded. Unfold them to their entire size, and place patterns accordingly. Use weights instead of pins.

- When placing pattern pieces, measure the distance from the fold to each end of the grainline arrow to ensure proper placement of the pattern.

sewing 101

Place pattern tracing material under slippery fabrics. Then place the pattern on top, and cut through all layers. The pattern tracing material keeps the fabric from slipping while cutting.

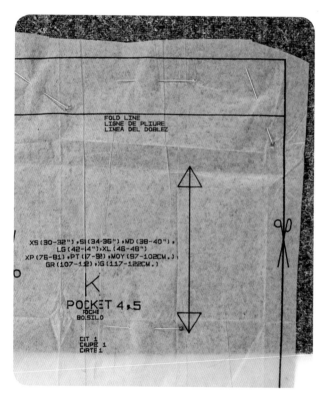

Place all pattern pieces on the fabric so the top of each piece is going the same direction.

EASIEST FABRICS

Broadcloth and Chambray

These fabrics are densely woven, soft and durable. They are easy fabrics for beginners to work with as irregularities are hard to see. Similar fabrics are gingham, cotton flannel, muslin, percale and denims. Prepare by washing and drying at least three times for shrinkage. Before washing, serge or zigzag the raw edges to prevent fraying.

Batiste

Batiste is lightweight and soft, and is made from cotton, wool, polyester or blends. Similar fabrics are dotted Swiss, eyelet, pima cotton, calico and lawn. Preshrink before cutting and sewing. To prevent stitching problems, use a straight-stitch needle plate.

Cotton

Cotton is available in a variety of fabric types, widths, patterns and weights. It is also a component of other fabrics such as broadcloth, calico, homespun, muslin, monk's cloth and canvas. Prepare by washing and drying at least three times for shrinkage.

Felt

Felt is wool and synthetic fibers that are pounded, pressed, shrunk and felted. It has no visible grain and doesn't fray. Both sides are the same, so mark the wrong side with pins or chalk. It can stretch out of shape.

Fleece

Fleece is a double-napped knit fabric that doesn't fray. It creates excess lint, so clean the sewing machine periodically while sewing. When topstitching, increase the stitch length.

Knit

Knits are easy to sew and fit, and require no pressing. The degree of stretch can be 10–100 percent, depending on the type of knit. Double knits can stretch 10 percent, jerseys from 20–25 percent, stretch terry and velour can stretch 50 percent, and swimwear and ribbing can stretch 50–100 percent. Choose a pattern that requires stretch and purchase the suggested knits.

sewing 101

When sewing a lightweight cotton fabric, using the appropriate-weight stabilizer helps prevent puckering. Alternatively, place a thin paper, such as tracing paper, under the fabric when sewing, and then pull the paper away.

Net and Tulle

Open net fabric is transparent and won't fray. If cutting multiple layers, securely pin the fabric together. Use a roller foot or wide presser foot when sewing to prevent catching on the fabric. Place stabilizer between fabric and feed dogs to prevent stitch problems.

Nylon and Polyester

These fabrics are strong, durable and available in various weights. Both dull needles quickly, so change needles often. Use a wide presser foot and a straight-stitch needle plate. If puckering occurs, hold the fabric firmly behind and in front of the needle.

Rayon

Rayon can be made to look like cotton, wool, silk or linen. It tends to fray, so finish raw edges with a serger, or an overcast or zigzag stitch. When buying, check the bolt for shrinkage amounts, and wash and dry accordingly. It may waterspot when wet, so test a small piece before washing the entire yardage. Wash in cold water and hang to dry. Press out wrinkles from the wrong side using a press cloth. Do not wring or twist.

sewing 101

In 1910, rayon was first called "artificial silk."

Sweatshirt

Sweatshirt fabrics are medium-weight to heavyweight knits. They have a napped surface, so lay out the pattern pieces according to the nap direction. Test the fabric before using—some shrink about 25 percent in both length and width.

Terry Cloth and Velour

Terry cloth has uncut loops on one or both sides, and velour looks like velveteen. Fold these fabrics with wrong sides together to cut; this "locks" the loops together for minimal slippage. If velour has uncut loops on both sides, cut through a single layer. To prevent stitching problems, use a wide presser foot or a zipper foot to stitch over bulky, uneven seams.

Tricot

Tricot is a knit with vertical ribs on one side and horizontal ribs on the other. It is available in various weights. Tricot doesn't shrink, but washing before cutting can prevent stitch problems. Washing removes the finish, thus eliminating skipped stitches. As both sides look like the "right" side, stretch crosswise; the edge will roll toward the right side of the fabric.

Woolen

Made with short yarn fibers, woolen has a "hairy" appearance. Some examples are tweeds, textured wools, washable wools and flannels. Cut through a single layer, and use a nap layout.

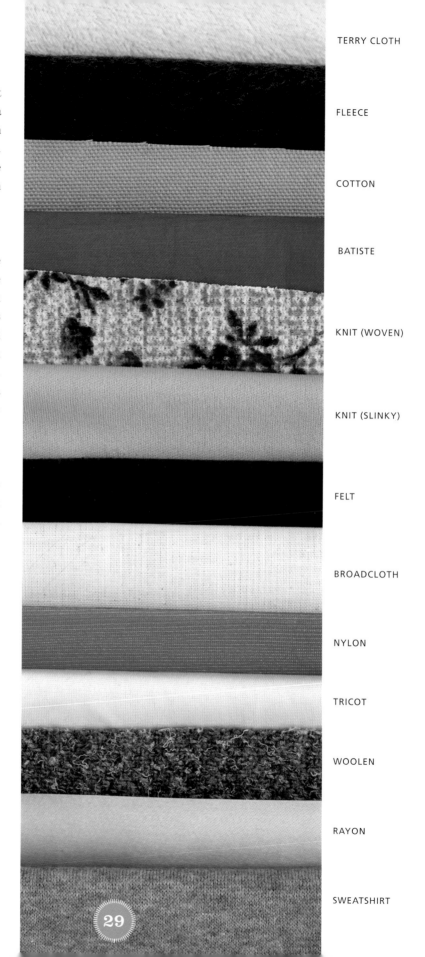

TERRY CLOTH

FLEECE

COTTON

BATISTE

KNIT (WOVEN)

KNIT (SLINKY)

FELT

BROADCLOTH

NYLON

TRICOT

WOOLEN

RAYON

SWEATSHIRT

CHALLENGING FABRICS

Chiffon

Chiffon is a lightweight, sheer fabric made from cotton, silk or synthetic fibers. It frays easily so finish edge seams with a serger, a zigzag stitch or (preferably) binding. Lay fabric in a single layer on pattern tracing material before cutting. Pin only in seam allowances as pins leave holes in fabric, or use weights to hold the pattern on the fabric. Use sharp shears to cut. Sew with a fine, sharp needle.

Gabardine

Gabardine is made from worsted wool, cotton or blends; it is a form of twill weave. One side is smooth, the other side has a diagonally ribbed surface. It resists wrinkles but is hard to press—the iron can leave imprints. It is also difficult to ease while sewing. Use nap layout. Cut seam allowances about one inch wide so they lay flat while sewing.

Georgette

Georgette is a fine, sheer crepe fabric made of silk, polyester or rayon. The textured and slippery nature makes it difficult to cut and sew. Before cutting, fold in half lengthwise and pin selvages. Pin only in seam allowances as pins leave holes in fabric, or use weights to hold the pattern on the fabric. Cut with very sharp shears. Always use new, sharp needles. A roller foot or a wide presser foot prevents creeping. When using a zigzag foot, layer tissue paper or water-soluble stabilizer between the fabric pieces while sewing. Georgette is a crisp fabric and wrinkle resistant.

Silk Crepe

Silk crepe is lightweight, slippery to sew, and has a crinkled surface. Cut and sew it like georgette. When sewing, gently pull fabric behind and in front of the needle to prevent puckered seams. Additional fabric types are poly crepe and satin-backed crepe.

Microfiber

Microfiber is made from manufactured fibers such as nylon, rayon, acrylic and polyester. Fabrics made from microfiber range from chiffon to insulating material. It tends to dull shears and needles very quickly, so plan to replace the needle frequently. Use needle sizes 60/8, 65/9 or 70/10. To keep fabric from slipping while cutting, place pins in selvage or use weights. Cut with very sharp shears. Sew with a roller foot, a wide presser foot or a zigzag foot. To control puckering, hold fabric taut in front and in back of the presser foot while sewing. Do not use a hot iron!

Satin

Satin varies from sheer and lightweight to heavyweight. Tighter weave satin has less fraying and less slippage. Lighter weight satin easily snags, is slippery and is prone to pin marks. Run your fingernail across the surface of the fabric—if yarn strands seem to separate, the fabric will fray, tend to pucker, and seams in areas of stress could be easily pulled out. Try cutting and sewing wide seam allowances.

Taffeta

Taffeta is made from silk, rayon, polyester, acetate or blends. Fabric creases easily and is marred by pin holes, so pin in seam allowances or use weights. Use very sharp shears and a very sharp needle. When necessary, use heat-away stabilizer. Press with a Teflon press mat; the stabilizer transfers from the fabric to the press mat and is easily removed. Seams tend to pucker when sewn, so hold fabric firmly behind and in front of the needle while sewing.

GABARDINE   GEORGETTE   CHIFFON   SATIN   SILK CREPE   MICROFIBER   TAFFETA

 ## sewing 101

- Silk is the only natural fiber that is naturally long. These long, fine fibers are known as *filament fibers*.

- Satin is characterized by its lustrous shine. It is made of warp yarns which "float" over the filling yarns, causing it to snag easily.

JUST PLAIN FUN FABRICS!

Faux Fur

Faux fur is a pile fabric and is available in various weights, pile depths and designs. Sewing distortions are easily hidden. It's bulky, so choose patterns with a minimal number of seams to reduce bulk. Cut through a single layer, positioning all pattern pieces in the same direction. Although not always noticeable, most faux furs have a nap direction. Sewing with a small zigzag stitch eliminates stitch holes (recommended: 2.5mm width, 0.5mm length). Use a roller foot or a walking foot to eliminate creeping.

sewing 101

Oil cloth was very popular in the 1950s in bold and colorful motifs. Similar fabric with vinyl on the front and cloth on the back can be found today. When sewing this fabric, try using a 90/14 needle, monofilament thread and a Teflon or walking foot.

Beaded, Embroidered or Sequined Fabric

These fabrics are embellished with beads and sequins, or sewn, fused or glued border designs. Cut through a single layer with right-side-up, and use nap layout. Check nap by running your hand down the fabric; sequins will lay flat in one direction. Avoid using fusible interfacing as fabric can be damaged by an iron.

Dupioni Silk

Dupioni silk may be soft or crisp, dull or radiant. It does fray considerably. Serge, zigzag stitch or overcast the edges after cutting for easier handling while sewing. If lightweight and slippery, lay on pattern tracing material before cutting to guarantee sharper cuts. Pins mar the fabric, so use weights instead.

Lamé Silk

Lamé silk contains lustrous shine and colors that appear to change. Metallic threads are woven into the fabric. It is available in various weights and does fray considerably.

DUPIONI SILK   FAUX FUR   LAMÉ SILK   EMBROIDERED FABRIC

CUTTING

Once fabric is cut, mistakes are difficult (or impossible) to correct. Cut carefully and accurately. As my carpenter grandfather always said, "Measure twice, cut once." Work on a flat surface. When cutting, never close the points of the shears: Cut almost to the tips, then slide the shears forward for another cut. Keep shears on the table at all times for accurate cuts. Cut precisely along the edge of the pattern's cutting line. Cut with the grain as much as possible. Don't turn fabric around to cut areas—walk around it instead.

sewing 101

Tailors and dressmakers have two different methods of cutting. Which are you?

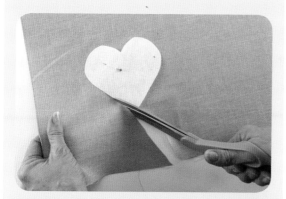

The tailor holds fabric in the left hand and shears in the right. This puts a little tension on the fabric, keeping it smooth while cutting.

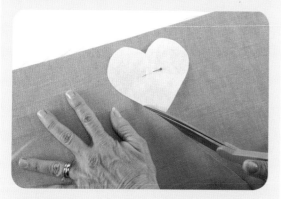

A dressmaker places the left hand on the fabric, close to the cutting line and the shears.

MARKING

As soon as you finish cutting, mark everything! There are many methods of marking—use one or a combination. Whenever possible, place marks directly on the fabric for accuracy.

Clips

Clip (straight cut) ⅛" (3.2mm) into the seam allowance. Notches (V-shaped cuts) will weaken the fabric, so make straight clips instead.

Chalk, Soap, Tailor's Chalk, Water-Soluble Pen

Colored chalk may leave a permanent stain, so try white chalk. Use soaps that don't have oil in them. Water-soluble pens may leave stains on fabrics that water spot easily. Test any of these on a small swatch before marking your fabric pieces.

Pins

Don't leave pins in the fabric too long or they may leave permanent holes. Some pins may even leave rust marks on the fabric if left for a long time.

Tailor's Tacks

Use white embroidery floss (colored floss may bleed into fabric) to mark. Sew long, droopy basting stitches along pattern lines. Snip between each stitch for easy removal later.

Tracing Wheel and Tracing Paper

Tracing wheels are available with serrated or smooth edges. Use a smooth edge tracing wheel when marking sheer fabrics. A serrated wheel can actually cut into the sheer fabric.

STITCHING

Even with the right needle, an appropriate thread and a clean machine, some fabrics are more challenging to sew a straight stitch in than others. Have you noticed puckering when sewing along the lengthwise grain? Fabric has very little give in this direction and tends to pucker. When sewing along the lengthwise grain of fabric, hold the fabric taut in back and in front of the needle. This prevents fabric from feeding too quickly. Be careful, though—don't tug or push, or you will break the needle.

The difference between a professional looking garment and one that is less-than-stellar is the stitching. Stitch length is based on fabric characteristics, and most importantly, the weight. Heavier fabrics require a longer stitch, and lighter fabrics behave best with a shorter stitch. Additionally, some fabrics such as leather may "stick" to the presser foot causing distorted stitches. Using a Teflon bottom foot or a light dusting of talcum powder helps.

Computerized machines automatically set the stitch length for medium-weight fabrics. Learn how to manually set your machine's stitch length and width to match the fabric when necessary.

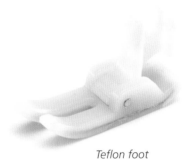

Teflon foot

Lightweight Fabrics (2mm–2.5mm stitch length)

- Longer stitches cause puckering. If a longer stitch length is needed, loosen the tension, and hold the fabric taut with one hand in front of the needle and one behind presser foot.

- Wide zigzag stitches tend to cause tunneling (pulling in from both sides of the seam line forming a ridge). Shorten the stitch length and narrow the stitch width.

- Use stabilizer or interfacing that's appropriate to fabric weight.

- Fabrics such as batiste tend to bunch up when starting to sew. Place a small piece of fabric or tear-away stabilizer under the foot, butting the edge of the batiste next to it. Begin sewing on the fabric scrap and continue onto the batiste.

- Crepe looks best when sewn with a stitch length of 2mm. Experiment on scrap fabric.

- When straight stitching, try using a zigzag foot with the needle in the far left or far right position.

Begin sewing on a fabric scrap and continue onto the batiste to prevent puckering at the beginning edge.

Mark the wrong side with chalk immediately after cutting the fabric. Marking each pattern piece eliminates confusion later.

Medium-Weight Fabrics
(2mm–3mm stitch length)

- If puckering occurs, lengthen the stitch to 3mm–3.5mm.
- Knit fabrics require a shorter stitch length of 1.5mm–2mm.
- Velvet has a nap and therefore requires a stitch length of 2mm–2.5mm.
- Ensure fabric is on grain with lengthwise and crosswise grains perpendicular to each other.
- If both sides look the same, mark the wrong side with chalk marks.

Heavyweight Fabrics
(2.5mm–4mm stitch length)

- *Very* heavyweight fabrics require a 3mm–4mm stitch length; a longer stitch can cause puckering.
- Use a higher number needle size to match a heavier thread, such as a higher number jeans needle.
- Use heavyweight, topstitching or embroidery thread.
- When sewing heavyweight wool, try a roller or walking foot.
- When sewing canvas and other heavyweight fabrics, a flat-felled seam is durable and eliminates fraying.
- A double thickness of heavyweight fabric may be too thick for regular pinning, so use paper clips or clothespins to hold fabric while sewing.
- A single layer hem reduces bulk.

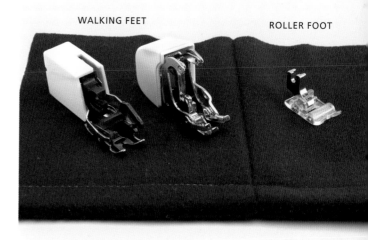

Use a roller or walking foot when sewing heavyweight wool or hard-to-sew slippery fabrics.

not just any straight pin

Don't use just any straight pin on your next sewing project! Be sure to use a quality pin that is the correct size. Select pins according to type of pin, pin head, length of pin, and even the type of metal used. Then, narrow down the remaining choices by choosing a pin based on length, shaft and point. Listed are just some of those pins from which you will be able to choose.

TYPES OF STRAIGHT PINS

Ball Point

Ball point pins have a rounded point designed for knits and lingerie fabrics. Use a long ball point pin for medium-weight knits.

Appliqué

Appliqué pins have a short length to help secure appliqué pieces.

Color Ball

Color ball pins are all-purpose pins for general sewing on medium-weight fabrics. An extra-long color ball pin is available for quilting and lofty fabrics.

Lace and Bridal

These are extra-fine pins for use on delicate fabrics and lace.

Dressmaker

Dressmaker pins are general-purpose pins suitable for use on medium-weight fabrics.

Glass Head

Glass head pins are general-purpose pins for use on medium-weight fabrics. They have a heat-resistant glass head. An extra-fine glass head pin is available for use on delicate fabrics.

Metallic

Metallic pins have a silver or gold plastic head. Use them for general sewing, decorative projects and crafts.

Pearlized

Pearlized pins have a colorful, pearlized head. Use them for general sewing, crafts, decorative projects and floral.

Quilting

Use these pins for basting quilt layers and pinning multiple layers of fabric. A long-length quilting pin also works especially well on furs, velvets, heavy trims and bulky fabrics.

Satin

Use these pins on satins and medium-weight fabrics. An extra-long satin pin has a long, tapered point.

Sequin

These pins are very short and designed for use on sequins, thin trims and hand appliqué.

Silk

Silk pins are rustproof and designed for use on silks and synthetic fabrics.

Flat-Flower Pins

These pins are easy to see, making it much less likely that you will leave one in the fabric or sew over them.

PIN BASICS

Choose the length of pin that will give you the best handling for your project. The pin should sufficiently secure the fabric, but should also be easy to handle.

• **Short**: ½"–⅞" (12.7mm–22.2mm) for detailed handwork and very close pinning.

• **Medium**: 1¹⁄₁₆"–1⁵⁄₁₆" (26.9mm–33.3mm) for multi-purpose, general use. Suitable for most projects.

• **Long**: 1½"–2" (38.1mm–50.8mm) for multiple layers of thick, lofty fabrics.

The shaft is the diameter of the pin body. Choose a pin shaft based on fabric type and weight.

• **0.5mm pins**: For sheer, lightweight fabrics.

• **0.6mm pins**: For medium-weight fabrics.

• **0.7mm–0.8mm pins**: For medium- to heavyweight fabrics.

Pins have various types of heads.

• **Metal**: small disk shapes

• **Plastic/nylon**: colored, pearlized or metal-colored balls

• **No-melt plastic**: flat flower or button shaped

• **Glass**: heat resistant balls

Pins are made from a variety of materials.

• **Nickel-plated steel**: rustproof and stick to magnetic pin cushions

• **Stainless steel**: rustproof

• **Brass**: rustproof

• **Nickel-plated brass**: rustproof and won't tarnish

Lastly, the point of the pin should slip easily into your fabric without creating large holes or snagging.

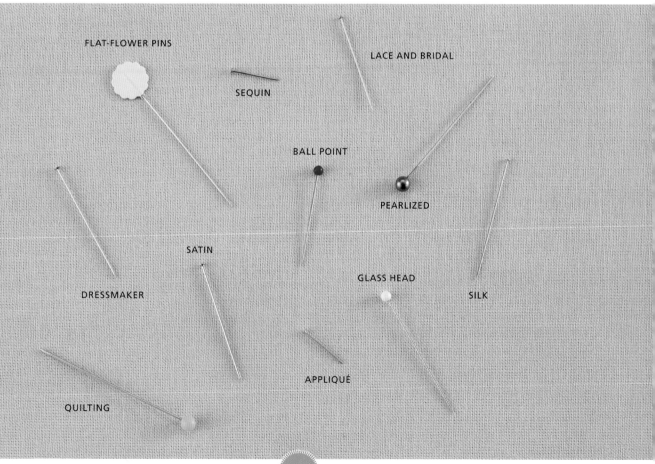

FLAT-FLOWER PINS

LACE AND BRIDAL

SEQUIN

BALL POINT

PEARLIZED

SATIN

DRESSMAKER

GLASS HEAD

SILK

APPLIQUÉ

QUILTING

stabilizers and interfacings

You have chosen your fabric with care, and have gathered appropriate needles and thread. To get a nice sharp, crisp stitch, especially when using built-in decorative stitches or sewing buttonholes, you will want to choose the proper stabilizer or interfacing to complete the job. Whether sewing a dense stitch or applying appliqué, using stabilizer or interfacing gives you professional results.

There are many types and forms of stabilizers and interfacings available. A general understanding of when to reach for which type not only improves the appearance of your sewing, but reduces frustration when stitches begin puckering or tunneling. Keep an ample supply of various types on hand. Practice with fabric scraps to determine the best one for the task at hand.

STABILIZERS

Stabilizers are meant to provide support, making fabric *stable*. They're designed to not give in any direction, holding fabric threads in place while stitching. With the machine's tug on the fabric eliminated, stitches come out crisp and stay secure. Using the proper stabilizer reduces puckering, thread breakage, stitch distortion, tunneling and skipped stitches. Stitches remain clear and crisp.

Stabilizers are used most often with densely formed stitching, like satin and decorative stitches. Use them regularly with appliqué, cutwork, monogramming and machine embroidery. When making buttonholes, use both stabilizer and interfacing for professional results. Reach for stabilizer when lightweight fabrics begin puckering.

There are four main types of stabilizers: tear-away, wash-away, heat-away and cut-away. They are available as fusible, nonfusible and adhesive-backed, and as woven and nonwoven. Which one you choose depends on the type of fabric and the stitch density. Experiment with several types to find the stabilizer best suitable for your project. Consider several factors to determine which to use: permanent or temporary support, weight of fabric, stitch density and visibility of the stabilizer.

There are a wide variety of stabilizers available. Choose the type that is most appropriate for your project and type of fabrics.

sewing 101

A *topper stabilizer* is a specific kind of stabilizer specifically for use on top of fabric to prevent loss of stitch detail in heavily napped fabrics, like terry cloth, corduroy, velvet and furs.

Tear-Away Stabilizer

Tear-away stabilizer provides temporary support of fabric. It is available from lightweight to heavyweight, and as fusible and nonfusible. If strong support is necessary, use multiple layers of lightweight stabilizer; this is easier to remove than a single layer of heavyweight stabilizer. Most are easy to remove, but take care not to pull the stitches. Test several types for ease in tearing in all directions. For very fine stitches, entredeux and fine lace, choose a stabilizer that tears easily without disturbing fine stitches. Any remaining stabilizer dissolves quickly in delicate washes.

Cut-Away Stabilizer

Cut-away stabilizer is permanent and provides durable support. It is available from light- to heavyweight, in black or white, fusible and nonfusible, woven and nonwoven. It has a high fiber content and doesn't break down under dense stitching. Trim away excess stabilizer after stitching, leaving about ¼" (6.4mm). Trim close to the stitching using sharp appliqué scissors. For more stability, layer two pieces with grains crossing at right angles.

Water-Soluble Stabilizer

Water-soluble stabilizer is a film or mesh designed to dissolve when wet, providing temporary support. It can be used as a backing or a topper. Use it when stitches will be visible from both sides. It's available from lightweight to heavyweight. If heavyweight is not available, layer two or three pieces to form a heavier, firmer stabilizer. Only use with fabrics that are washable. To remove, trim excess near stitches and soak in water, rinsing several times to eliminate all stabilizer. Save all those scraps! Place them between pressing cloths and press with an iron to fuse into a larger piece.

Heat-Away Stabilizers

Heat-away stabilizers are available as woven and plastic-like films. The plastic-like film works well as a topping, staying under the stitching to provide continual support. Use when permanent support is necessary after stitching. Remove excess stabilizer around stitching by touching with a dry (not steam) iron—the stabilizer turns brown, crumbles, and is easily brushed away. For easier cleanup, place the stitched item between two paper towels and press with an iron until brown. Then place the item in a resealable storage bag and roll in your hands to crumble the stabilizer. Dispose of the bag when finished.

Wash-Away Stabilizers

Wash-away stabilizers are available in liquids and sprays. They are perfect for heirloom stitching, and can be applied only where needed. Spray or brush on fabric and let dry. The stabilizer stiffens, providing a perfect base for sewing. Several light applications works better than a heavy application.

Adhesive-Backed Stabilizer

Adhesive-backed stabilizer is nonwoven and perfect for fabrics that tend to stretch, such as knits. It's ironed to the wrong side of fabric and is usually permanent. Once ironed, it gives a firm crispness to fabric. The adhesive backing can be hard on needles and thread, so slow down the sewing speed. Iron-on stabilizer is a perfect choice for most appliqué. Use iron settings to match the fabric.

Cut-Away Fusible Mesh

Cut-away fusible mesh is a lightweight nylon stabilizer with an embossed design, making it invisible. It can be sewn or fused for added support. Cut away any excess.

Water-Activated Stabilizer

Water-activated stabilizer works great for embroidery and for sewing on lightweight wovens and towels. Moisten the stabilizer and place where needed. After sewing, remoisten it and tear away the excess. The stabilizer can be moistened and repositioned if necessary.

INTERFACING

Interfacing is not as strong as stabilizer and is designed to move and give with the fabric. Areas of greatest stress, like buttonholes on heavyweight fabrics, benefit from using both interfacing and stabilizer. Don't be tempted to skip adding interfacing—it's one of the secret ingredients to a gorgeous garment. It gives shape, body and support ,and prevents stress, puckering and stretching.

There are three basic types of interfacing: woven, nonwoven and knit. Each is available as fusible or nonfusible. When choosing interfacing, no matter which type, it should always be a lighter weight than the fabric. Most interfacing is available from lightweight to heavyweight. Consider making a small sample to test the compatability of a specific fabric and interfacing.

When choosing interfacing, ask yourself the following questions:

- Does the interfacing give enough body? Too much?
- How does it feel—pliable, stiff?
- Is there color bleed from the fusible? Lumps? Bubbles?
- Are the care requirements the same for both the interfacing and the fabric?
- Do both the interfacing and the fabric *give* in the same directions?
- Does the interfacing show through the fabric?

Whichever interfacing you choose, make sure it is a lighter weight than your fabric.

Woven Interfacing
Woven interfacing is made of fibers woven together, and has exceptional drape when cut on the bias. It tends to be stronger than nonwoven. Uses are generally for facings, lapels or any area needing stability and extra body.

Nonwoven Interfacing
Nonwoven interfacing is made from man-made fibers pressed together. There isn't any grain or fraying, so pattern pieces can be placed in any direction. It can be used on most fabrics and is available as both fusible and nonfusible.

Knit Fusible Interfacing
Knit fusible interfacing is flexible and lightweight, giving permanent support to the fabric. Use to stabilize decorative stitching, plackets, buttonholes and garment edges.

sewing 101

Needles become coated with resin when sewing fusibles or when using temporary basting spray. Clean the needle with a cotton ball dipped in alcohol, but don't get alcohol on your sewing machine. Change your needle frequently.

PRESHRINKING INTERFACING

Preshrinking interfacing, both fusible and nonfusible, takes a bit of time, but with this initial preparation, you will never be surprised after the first washing. A large tub, sink or bathtub is necessary. Lay the interfacing with gentle folds in the tub and add hot water to just cover. Let it soak until the water has cooled. Lay the interfacing on a large towel. Roll up the towel, gently squeezing out the excess water from the interfacing. Don't twist the towel. Then place the interfacing on a flat surface until dry. After preshrinking, I roll mine on cardboard tubes to store until ready to use.

Some fusible interfacing instructions recommend a steam-shrink technique before application. Cut the interfacing slightly larger than the desired size and shape. Place the glue side down onto wrong side of the fabric. Set the iron on the "wool" setting and hold above (not on) the interfacing to lightly steam the surface. The interfacing may shrink slightly. Cover with a press cloth and fuse as directed.

FUSING TIPS

- Preshrink both fabric and interfacing to prevent bubbling on one side and shrinkage on the other.

- A low iron setting prevents bubbling on both interfacing and fabric.

- Before fusing, warm the fabric by pressing with steam. This eliminates wrinkles and removes any remaining shrinkage.

- If you don't have a steam iron or your iron produces too little steam to fuse, use a damp cloth to create steam.

- Press—don't iron—for a wrinkle-free application.

- When fusing, if resin bleeds through the fabric, use a lighter interfacing or a sew-in type.

- If interfacing lines show through the fabric, try a lighter interfacing or pink the interfacing edges before fusing.

- Which to use in your sewing project? If unsure, test both fusible and sew-in interfacing before using.

Test Fusible Interfacing

Cut 3" (8cm) square pieces of fusible interfacing options. Fuse each to a piece of the fabric you are using. Wash and dry the sample as you would the fabric. Think about the tips and questions on page 40 to determine which test piece is appropriate for your project.

Test Sew-In Interfacing

Sandwich a layer of interfacing between two pieces of the fabric you are using. Think about the tips and questions on page 40 to determine which test piece is appropriate for your project.

Test fusible interfacing

Test sew-in interfacing

demystifying your machine

Time to take control of your sewing machine! Spending a few minutes on general maintenance after each sewing project will save you time and frustration later. Feeling comfortable with your sewing? Move beyond using utility feet and try a few specialty feet and new techniques. Your sewing time will continue to be creative and enjoyable!

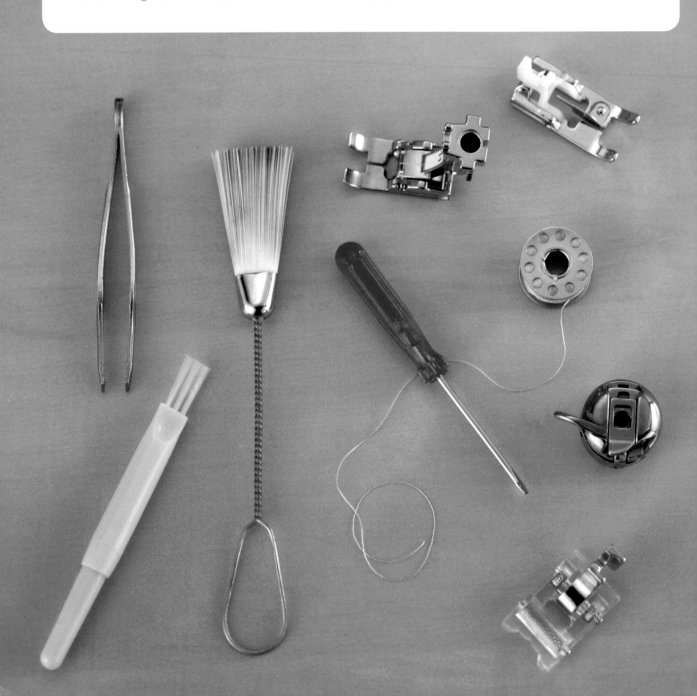

general maintenance

A few minutes of cleaning at the end of each project can prevent many machine and stitching problems. Just running fabric under the needle creates lint, and if you are not using quality thread, even more lint is accumulating in your machine every time you sew. Lint settles in the bobbin area, around the feed dogs and even in the tension discs. Simply covering the machine when it's not in use keeps out dust, lint and hair. Computerized machines especially benefit from covering to protect the printed circuit board.

CLEANING

Since many sewing problems are caused by lint, dust and lodged pieces of thread, a good rule is to clean the machine at the first sign of stitch problems. A daily brushing of lint and dirt is preventive maintenance. Lint, dirt and threads build up in various parts of the machine and become drenched with oil and lubricant. This gummy mess wreaks havoc on your machine and is frustrating for you.

Use the nylon lint brush that came with the machine. I keep a narrow paint brush by each machine for quick cleaning. Each time you change bobbin thread, give the bobbin area a quick cleaning. Fluff out the brush and each bristle will reach and catch the dust much better. A pair of tweezers easily grabs stray pieces of thread hiding in and around the feed dogs and bobbin area.

Remove and throw away the needle. Remove the presser foot, needle plate and bobbin case. If your machine has a hook race, remove it also. Using the lint brush, clean under the feed dogs and around the bobbin area. Blow dislodged dirt outwards with compressed air.

Keep tweezers on hand to fish out rogue threads from the bobbin area.

Check the machine's manual for oiling places. If in doubt about oiling your machine, check with your machine mechanic.

If your machine continues to have problems, take it to a sewing machine repair shop. Be sure to have them give a good cleaning to areas you don't normally attend.

Follow your manual's instructions or ask your machine mechanic to show you general cleaning methods for your specific machine. Always start at the top and work down the machine, moving dust downwards.

sewing 101

Never blow into your machine—your breath contains moisture.

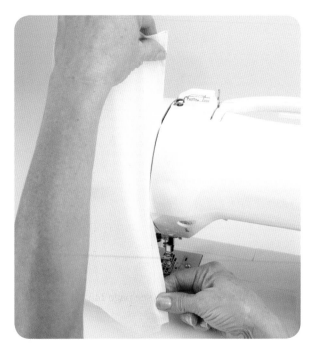

Use a piece of muslin to clean the tension discs.

When the tension is too tight, the bottom thread is pulled up to the top side of the fabric. Too little upper thread is fed through, causing seams to pucker and thread to break easily.

When the tension is too loose, the upper thread is pulled down to the bottom side of the fabric. Too much thread passes through, resulting in weak seams that can easily pull apart.

Test upper and lower tension before each project or when adding a new foot or thread type. To test, use one color in the bobbin and another color feeding through the top—this helps you quickly recognize balanced tension. When testing specialty thread, decorative stitches or a satin stitch, always place tear-away stabilizer under the fabric or between a folded piece of fabric to replicate regular sewing.

To test, cut a 6" (15cm) square of fabric. Fold the fabric on the bias and stitch ½" (12.7mm) from the fold. Are stitches balanced on both top and bottom? Did puckering occur? Hold both ends of the fabric between your thumb and index finger, one at each end of the stitching line. Pull on the stitching with quick, even force until one of the threads breaks. If the upper thread broke, the upper tension is too loose. If both threads break (when using considerable force), both tensions are balanced.

TENSION DISCS

While tension discs are easily seen on older machines, the area is quite hidden on newer ones. Raise the presser foot to relieve tension. Fold a piece of clean muslin and gently slide it into the tension discs to dislodge dust and lint. Use a can of compressed air to blow out the dust and lint that dislodges. Be sure to blow everything out and away from the machine, not back into it.

TEST FOR BALANCED TENSION

Keeping a balanced tension is a major component for perfect stitches. The needle and thread come together to make a stitch, but the tension allows the correct amount of thread to pass through the machine and to the bobbin. Maintaining balanced tension pressure is key so that the same amount of thread flows from the spool and the bobbin simultaneously.

Hold both ends of the fabric between your thumb and index finger, one at each end of the stitching line. Pull on the stitching with quick, even force until one of the threads breaks.

Your machine may have automatic tension and you will rarely need to touch the tension adjuster for most of your regular sewing. There are times, however, when you will need to manually adjust the tension. Sewing silks, knits or with specialty threads may require tension adjustment. Additionally, using a specialty sewing foot can require adjustment.

When adjusting tension, put the presser foot down and have the machine threaded. To increase tension, move to a higher number. To decrease, adjust to a lower number.

ADJUSTING BOBBIN TENSION

Rarely does bobbin tension need to be adjusted for regular sewing. You will, however, need to adjust when using a thicker thread such as pearl cotton or ribbon. Bobbins have a spring screw which regulates tension on the thread.

Before adjusting bobbin tension, check:

- **Threading**: Recheck the thread path. Does the thread move smoothly through all guides? Be sure to thread with the presser foot up, which releases the upper tension and allows thread to move properly through all guides and tension. Check that thread is moving freely and not snagging. Be sure there is not a burr on the spool of thread, and that the spool is placed on the spool pin to unwind correctly (see page 19). If using a bobbin of thread on the spool pin, it may not unwind smoothly.

- **Lint:** Dirt and lint cause many stitch problems. Check the bobbin area for lint and thread ends. Use a lightweight, lint-free cloth to clean in and around the bobbin area. If using a can of air to spray out lint, remember to spray outward.

- **Improperly filled bobbin:** Remove all remaining thread from a bobbin before filling with new thread. Wind at a consistent speed according to the manual instructions. Wind nylon threads slowly or by hand to prevent them from stretching. When winding heavier, specialty threads, wind slowly. Only use a bobbin designed for your machine. The wrong bobbin can cause skipped stitches, thread breakage or machine damage.

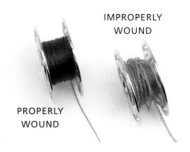

Make sure the bobbin is wound smoothly and consistently for optimal results.

- **Damaged parts**: Check that the needle is not bent. Check for any burrs along the thread path in the tension, thread guides, needle plate, presser foot, bobbin case, bobbin area or take-up lever.

- **Fabric, thread and needle**: Use the needle size appropriate for thread and fabric (see page 145). If the needle hole is too large or too small, thread will not pass through, nor stitch properly. Change to a larger or smaller needle as necessary.

- **Using heavyweight thread**: If stitch problems occur, loosen the upper thread tension. This allows heavier bobbin thread to lie flat on the surface of the fabric. Since the heavier threads will not penetrate the fabric, this may be the only adjustment necessary. If stitching is still inferior, bypass the bobbin thread tension following the instruction manual.

Only as a last resort, adjust the bobbin case tension screw. Follow instructions in your sewing machine manual. When adjusting the bobbin tension, do so in quarter increments. This makes it easier to return to the original position.

Adjust the bobbin case tension screw only after you have tried everything else.

TEST BOBBIN TENSION

If your machine has a removable bobbin case, you can test bobbin tension by holding the thread tail and letting the case dangle, giving thread a quick jerk. Does the case slip down easily? The thread should support the weight of the bobbin and the case. If the thread slips down, tighten the bobbin screw about a quarter of a turn. Thread the machine and test sew to check the stitch quality.

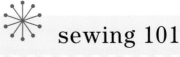

sewing 101

Purchase a second bobbin case to use for specialty threads. Adjustments can be made to this bobbin case while still maintaining factory tension on your regular bobbin case.

BYPASS BOBBIN THREAD TENSION

For any type of specialty bobbin work, the bobbin tension should be loosened or bypassed completely. Some machines have a wider slot on the side of the bobbin case that allows thicker threads to pass through; on these cases, the bobbin tension need only be slightly adjusted. Other machines may have a special bobbin available with a *pigtail* or *finger* (wire hole) to insert thread. If your bobbin does not accommodate thicker threads, there are several other methods to try depending on your machine model.

• Loosen the bobbin tension spring by quarter turns until the thread flows smoothly.

• Machines that do not have a bobbin case: Place the bobbin in the bobbin hole without placing the thread through the bobbin tension. Let the bobbin thread hang freely. Pull the bobbin thread up as you do normally.

• Machines with a bobbin case: Don't put the thread through the tension spring of the bobbin case. Let the bobbin thread hang freely. Pull the bobbin thread up as normal.

Test bobbin tension by holding the thread tail and letting the case dangle.

TENSION CONTROL

A machine's stitching should be smooth with even stitches on the top and bottom of the fabric. The upper needle thread is controlled by thread guides and the tension dial located on the upper part of the machine. Even if your machine has automatic tension control, there are times when the tension needs to be tweaked. Fabrics such as leather and denim will require a different setting than delicate fabrics. Thread weight also makes a difference on tension setting. Grab some scraps before beginning a project and test different tension settings until you have the best one for your fabric and thread. Jot notes in your journal; over time, you will have a record of the correct tension on various projects.

To adjust the tension, turn the regulator dial located at the top of the machine. If yours is a numeric dial, it may go from 1–10—from loosest to tightest. Just remember, the lower the number, the looser the tension.

If the tension is too tight, turn the dial to a lower number and test the stitch. Lower the dial and retest if necessary. If the thread is too loose and appears crooked, the tension may be too loose. Turn the dial to a higher number and test the stitch. Repeat if necessary until a perfect stitch is formed.

Whether your machine's tension dial moves up and down or from side to side, all machines basically have the same four components to control tension—thread guides, tension discs, regulator for upper thread and bobbin case spring for bobbin thread.

The average tension setting can be marked differently on various sewing machine models.

sewing 101

Does the fabric suddenly begin to pucker while sewing? The tension may have changed. Stop and check all the thread guides—the thread may have "jumped" out of one. Rethread properly and continue sewing.

WHEN TO LOOSEN, WHEN TO TIGHTEN?

- Loosen tension when blind hem stitching begins to pull and pucker.

- Loosen tension to prevent fagoting stitches from pulling the two sides together.

- Loosen tension to pull the upper thread to the underside (creating a nice raised effect) when making buttonholes, satin stitching and for some decorative stitching.

- Loosen tension to reduce tunneling.

- Loosen tension to reduce puckering when sewing on the lengthwise grain of fabric.

- Tighten tension to enhance the raised effect of twin pin tucks. Loosen when puckering occurs.

- Tighten tension to perfect hemstitching holes. Loosen when puckering occurs.

- Tighten tension to automatically make gathers.

putting the right foot forward

There are as many types of presser feet as there are sewing tasks. Some are utilitarian, such as the zipper and blindhem foot, while others help add creative touches, such as the couching foot. Using the right foot improves stitching appearance and reduces time spent on tedious tasks.

Each foot is specially designed for a specific job. Knowing which foot to reach for frees up your time for more creativity. The foot might be designed to hold cording securely under the machine needle or to accurately stitch very close to edges. Although not often looked at when selecting which foot to use, the underside of each foot is crucial for the proper feeding of fabrics. For example, a straight-stitch foot is flat on the bottom with a narrow opening, but a satin stitch foot has an indented bottom which allows fabric to move freely instead of bunching up over the dense stitching. When adding pin tucks to a project, grab the grooved pin-tuck foot for perfectly straight lines.

Take advantage of the many feet available. You'll achieve professional results and save time.

INTERCHANGEABLE FEET

Snap-On Feet

Most sewing machines made after the 1980s use snap-on feet. They are attached to the machine through a foot holder, also called a shank attachment. The foot holder is screwed onto the presser bar, with a lever on the back. At the bottom of the foot holder is a horizontal bar. Pushing the lever down removes and attaches the snap-on feet onto the bar. The length and width of this bar varies among manufacturers and machine models, so be sure to purchase the correct one for your machine.

Many machines with the snap-on foot can also use screw-on, low-shank feet. Rufflers, for example, rarely are made to snap-on; instead, they screw directly onto the presser bar. A quick and easy measure will let you know whether your snap-on foot can also utilize low-shank feet.

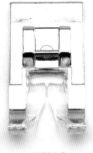

ZIPPER FOOT   ZIGZAG (ALL-PURPOSE) FOOT   OPEN TOE FOOT

Snap-on feet

Measure from the machine bed to the middle of the screw hole to determine the shank of your machine.

Low-shank foot adaptor

To check the shank of your machine, lower the presser foot and measure from the machine bed to the middle of the screw hole. If this distance measures ½" (12.7mm), your machine can use screw-on low-shank feet as well as snap-on feet.

Feet for BERNINA, Kenmore, Janome, Baby Lock and other machine models may have a shank designed to specifically fit that machine type. For most of these machines, if you need to use a low-shank foot, check to see if a low-shank foot adaptor is available for your machine.

Screw-On Feet

Machines made prior to the 1980s most likely have a screw-on foot, either low-, high- or slant-shank. It is important to determine which shank your machine has because only those feet will fit. To remove and add a new foot, remove the regular presser foot by loosening the screw to the left of the machine's foot. Attach the new foot and tighten the screw. If your machine is a low-shank, you may be able use snap-on feet. To do so, purchase a snap-on presser foot holder that fits your machine.

Whenever placing a new foot on your sewing machine, always ensure the needle clears the opening. If your machine has an adjustable needle position, also check to see if the needle is clear when moving it right or left of center.

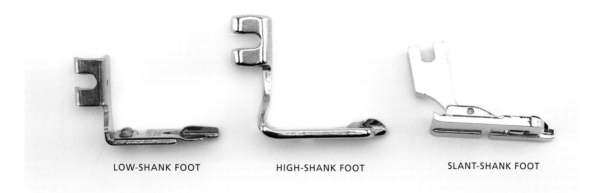

LOW-SHANK FOOT   HIGH-SHANK FOOT   SLANT-SHANK FOOT

Various presser foot shank sizes

NARROW HEMMER

SHELL HEMMER

ROLLED HEMMER

STRAIGHT STITCH

ZIGZAG (SATIN STITCH)

OPEN-TOE (APPLIQUÉ)

ZIPPER

BUTTONHOLE

BUTTON SEW-ON

BLINDSTITCH (BLIND HEM)

UTILITY FEET

Each basic utility foot is specifically designed for certain sewing tasks, helping you save time and achieve a professional finish. Most are numbered or lettered for easy identification. Your feet may look slightly different than those pictured, but once you've identified and learned to use them, you will wonder what you did without them!

Straight-Stitch Foot

This foot is suitable for all fabrics. It keeps fabric together and flat without puckering. The bottom of the foot is flat for consistent contact with feed dogs. A very small needle hole accommodates a straight stitch only—not zigzag or decorative stitches. When sewing a straight stitch on lightweight fabrics, the narrow opening prevents fabric from being shoved into the needle plate hole.

Zigzag (Satin Stitch) Foot

This foot has a wide needle hole to accommodate left and right needle swings and a groove underneath that allows dense stitching to pass easily under the foot. Use it for appliqué, cut work, decorative edges, attaching ribbon and monogramming. Some manufacturers may use the zigzag foot as the all-purpose sewing foot.

Hemmer Foot

There are three types of hemmer feet, each with a specific purpose. Manufacturers may also offer a multi-functional hemmer.

- **Narrow hemmer:** Designed to fold the fabric over twice and sew it down flat using a straight stitch. There are three sizes; the groove on the bottom correlates to the hemmer size and the final hem size.

- **Shell hemmer:** Folds the fabric over twice, and is used in conjunction with a zigzag, overlock, or blind stitch to form tiny scallops.

- **Rolled hemmer:** Folds the fabric over twice, and is used in conjunction with a zigzag stitch to produce a raised, rounded hem called a rolled-and-whipped hem.

Open-Toe (Appliqué) Foot

This foot is completely open in front of the needle, increasing stitch visibility. It has a groove underneath that allows dense stitching to pass easily under the foot. Since the foot doesn't have firm contact with the feed dogs, it moves relatively freely, making it easier to turn curves on appliqué. Use it with fabric that has sufficient stabilizer to keep it stiff.

Blindstitch (Blind Hem) Foot

This foot is used primarily for sewing invisible hems on medium- to heavyweight cottons, wool and blended fabrics. Used in conjunction with the blind hem stitch on the sewing machine, a guide on the foot keeps stitches aligned with the folded fabric edge. It is also useful for hem stitching lace and for topstitching.

Zipper Foot

This foot is slim and narrow, and is designed to sew close to zipper coils. The centered toe provides maximum contact with the feed dogs, while the adjustable needle position keeps the stitching close to the zipper coils. (If an adjustable needle position is unavailable on your machine, use an adjustable zipper foot.) When sewing *invisible* zippers, use an invisible zipper foot. Its grooves allow the zipper coils to pass directly under the foot. You can also use this foot to sew close to piping and cording and to attach tape strips.

(continued on page 52...)

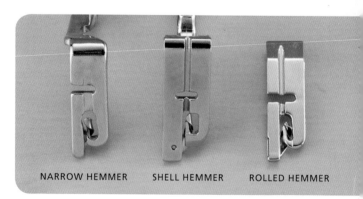

NARROW HEMMER   SHELL HEMMER   ROLLED HEMMER

The bottoms of hemmer feet

Button Sew-On Foot

This foot is designed to hold buttons securely while sewing. Some button sew-on feet have an adjustable pin mounted to the front for sewing thread shanks. Use it in conjunction with the zigzag stitch to attach buttons, snaps, hook and eyes, and bows.

Buttonhole Foot

This foot has a raised sole that allows smooth movement over built-up threads. Some have automatic sensors and others are controlled manually. Machines have a wide range of built-in buttonhole styles to help achieve professional buttonholes.

SPECIALTY FEET

Attach a specialty foot to your machine and begin broadening the techniques you can master with your machine. Add elaborate embellishments or a perfectly scalloped hem to your next sewing project. After some initial practice, you will find many more uses for each foot!

Pin-Tuck Foot

The pin-tuck foot is designed with grooves on the bottom to form evenly spaced twin-needle pin tucks. The foot comes with three, five, seven or nine grooves. The larger the number, the smaller the groove and space between grooves. The three-groove foot has 3mm grooves running the length of the sole. The seven- and nine-groove feet are helpful when sewing lightweight fabrics and heirloom stitching. Pin-tuck feet are also used for stitching cording or corded edges.

Cording Foot

The three-and five-groove cording feet are designed to couch multiple strands of cording simultaneously, holding them side by side. The slots in front of the foot prevent tangling and twisting as cords move under the needle. The sole of the foot has a large cut-out section so cords and dense stitches move freely. The three-groove foot has three slots for thicker cording, while the five-groove foot has five slots perfect for thinner cords.

Appliqué Foot (Embroidery Foot)

The appliqué foot (also called an embroidery foot) is suitable for stitching fine, lightweight fabrics as it provides the extra stabilization needed for proper stitching. It is designed for satin stitching with a wedge-shaped groove underneath, which allows dense satin stitches to pass freely. The wedge is wider at the back to aid sewing around appliqué curves and shapes. Some appliqué feet have a small thread guide on the front allowing narrow cord or elastic to pass directly down the center of the foot while sewing. A clear appliqué foot allows greater visibility of the stitching line while sewing.

Piping Foot

The piping foot is suitable for stitching heavy braids, trims, piping and beads. Trims fit into a grooved channel underneath the foot, keeping them securely in place and directly under the needle while sewing. Some have a ridge under the left side which serves as a guide for the piping edge. It is useful for straight and curved piping edges. For many machines, this foot is available in $\frac{1}{8}$" (3.2mm) and $\frac{3}{16}$" (4.8mm) widths. Choose a foot according to the thickness of trim being used. A welting foot has similar applications.

Roller Foot

The roller foot allows easy sewing of hard-to-sew fabrics, such as leathers, vinyls, silk, microfibers and other fabrics that tend to creep. The textured rollers actually roll along the fabric, preventing it from shifting and eliminating damage from impressions. A roller foot also works effectively when appliquéing on suede or when sewing velvets.

(continued on page 54...)

RUFFLER

CORDONNET

FREE-MOTION COUCHING

PIPING (SCREW ON)

APPLIQUÉ (EMBROIDERY)

ROLLER

TAILOR TACK (FRINGE)

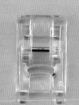

PIPING (SNAP ON)

EDGESTITCH

CORDING

PIN-TUCK

BRAIDING

Free-Motion Couching Foot

No matter which direction you wish to sew, the free-motion couching foot keeps cords, ribbons and braids directly under the needle. Feed the trim through the guide on the top of the foot, and down through the needle hole. Allow the trim to feed smoothly while sewing, and any design can be precisely sewn.

Cordonnet (Topstitching) Foot

The cordonnet foot is designed to use with topstitching thread or heavy buttonhole twist, adding designer touches to your project. A groove under the foot allows heavy threads to pass freely after stitches have been formed. The groove tapers to the back for easy maneuverability and secure fabric control. Use this foot to couch heavy yarns, for passementerie, or to satin stitch over wire for decorative trims.

Braiding Foot

Use the braiding foot to couch over narrow braid. The braid is fed through a center hole in the presser foot, which keeps it directly under the needle. Couching stitches fall perfectly on either side of the the braid. A groove underneath the foot accommodates the thickness of the braid.

sewing 101

Some manufacturers offer nonstick feet for sewing over difficult fabrics, eliminating any drag on the fabric. These feet slide smoothly over the fabric while stitching. Nonstick feet can be found for the straight, zigzag, zipper and open embroidery functions.

Edgestitch Foot

Use this foot for perfectly placed stitching along edges and seams. The foot has a metal blade to guide the fabric when stitching along an edge or near a seamline. The blade (guide) is located only in front of the foot to allow maneuverability when stitching around curved edges and to use as a reference for sewing straight seam lines. Use it when stitching in the ditch, sewing on lace and ribbons, or even when sewing tucks.

Tailor Tack (Fringe) Foot

The original intention of the tailor tack foot was to eliminate the tedious job of marking pattern pieces with hand tailor tacks. This foot can still be used to mark seamlines, darts and notches. Used in conjunction with at least a ⅛" (3mm) zigzag stitch, tack marks are quickly sewn and just as quickly removed.

A tall metal ridge falls in the center of the foot. The zigzag stitch forms over the ridge, causing the thread to form a loop on the fabric. Use this foot for tailor tacks and to create other decorative stitches. Adjust tension lower or higher to achieve different looks to the zigzag stitch, as well as to sew on buttons, add fagoting, make fringe and to create other textural effects.

Ruffler Foot

The ruffler is a true time-saver when sewing yards and yards of pleated or gathered fabric. The foot actually creates pleats, yet when adjusted to fall close together, the pleats are ruffled. An adjustment lever on the front of the foot sets the frequency for a pleat with every stitch, every sixth stitch or every twelfth stitch. Setting the lever at "zero" allows you to straight stitch with no pleats.

common stitch problems, causes and solutions

Every sewer runs into an occasional puckered seam or dropped stitch. Nothing is more frustrating than happily sewing along—until the needle breaks! You replace the needle—and it breaks again. Or the thread breaks and no matter how many times you rethread, it breaks again. You try adjusting tension up, down, and up again but nothing solves the problem.

Knowing what the problem might be and troubleshooting methods to try goes a long way toward enjoying all your sewing time. For a needle that continually breaks, you might first check the needle for damage, check the threading path, or check for trapped lint in the feed dogs or bobbin area. Surprisingly, the most common causes of sewing problems are improper threading, a dirty machine and a damaged needle.

SKIPPED STITCHES

Are skipped stitches raising your frustration level? The needle could be the cause of the problem. It might be an improper type or size, or it might possibly be damaged and moving roughly through the fabric. The needle could be covered with residue from fabric sizing, or it might even have lint on it. Although not easily seen, fabric clings to the needle each time it goes through the hole in the needle plate. With the thread so close to the needle, if there is a problem with the needle, it can't make a loop large enough for the shuttle hook to catch and create the stitch.

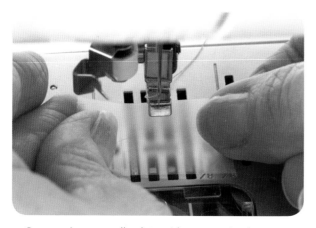

Cover a zigzag needle plate with tape to simulate a straight-stitch needle plate. Then poke a needle hole in the tape.

- Needle may be bent or damaged. Replace with a new one.

- Needle may be the incorrect size or type. Replace to match fabric type and thread size.

- Thread take-up lever has not been threaded. Rethread, ensuring thread goes through all guides.

- Bobbin may be low on thread. Check and replace with a full bobbin.

- Tension may be too tight. Loosen slightly.

- Try a universal needle, a topstitching needle or a ballpoint depending on fabric.

- The needle may not be set properly. Reset, ensuring it is fully inserted.

- If sewing a straight stitch using a zigzag needle plate, the fabric may be penetrating the needle hole of the needle plate. Change to a straight-stitch plate. If not available, try covering the zigzag hole with tape and make a small hole in the tape for the needle.

- When sewing over different heights of fabric seams, the foot may not be level. Try holding the front toe down as you sew, or make a leveler out of cardboard to raise the foot to the height of the seam. Place the leveler behind and in front of the presser foot as needed while sewing. Check to see if there is a leveler for your machine.

NEEDLE BREAKS

- Needle may be too thin for the fabric. Replace with a larger size.

- Needle may not be inserted in the presser bar all the way. Replace with a new needle and make sure it's fully inserted.

- The presser foot may be the wrong one for the sewing task. If sewing a stitch that goes side to side, be sure the needle hole is wide enough to accommodate the needle without hitting the foot.

- Thread may be tangling around the spool. Untangle and ensure the thread pulls from behind the spool of thread. Check for burrs on the thread spool and along the thread path. Use a spool cap.

- The bobbin may be inserted incorrectly, or not at all.

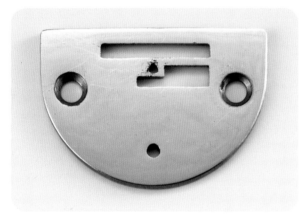

Check your needle plate! Shown is a straight-stitch needle plate. Never use a straight-stitch plate with a zigzag stitch.

UPPER THREAD BREAKS

- Tension may be too tight. Slightly loosen.

- Threading may be incorrect. Rethread.

- Needle may be bent or have a small burr. Replace with a new needle.

- Needle may be the wrong size or type. Check fabric type and thread size for proper needle.

- Thread quality may be poor; it may have a knot in it. Rethread with higher quality thread.

- Thread take-up lever may not be threaded. Rethread.

- Areas the thread passes over may be damaged (thread guides, tension, take-up lever, etc.). Check for noticeable damage, and take to repair center for further troubleshooting.

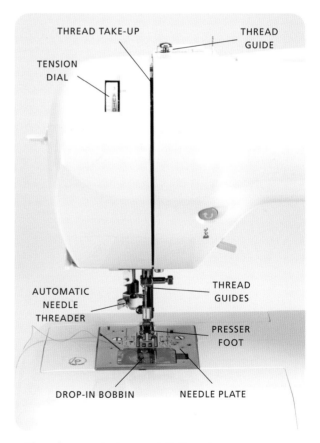

THREAD TAKE-UP

THREAD GUIDE

TENSION DIAL

AUTOMATIC NEEDLE THREADER

THREAD GUIDES

PRESSER FOOT

DROP-IN BOBBIN

NEEDLE PLATE

Threading may be incorrect. Rethread.

BOBBIN THREAD BREAKS

- Bobbin may not be wound properly. Remove bobbin and check for gaps in the thread.

- Bobbin may not be inserted correctly. Remove and reinsert, checking that the bobbin is firmly in place. If your bobbin has a bobbin case, make sure you hear hear the "click."

- Lint may be caught in bobbin area. Remove the bobbin, clean the bobbin and bobbin case area, and add oil. Follow manufacturer's manual for proper cleaning and oiling.

- Bobbin may not be in the machine. Remove the tangled stitches and insert the bobbin.

- Bobbin case may not be threaded correctly. Be sure thread is inserted into slot. (This also controls the bobbin tension.)

- Needle plate may be damaged. Remove it and feel for any rough areas. Small burrs can be rubbed out with a very fine polishing cloth.

Be sure thread is securely inserted into slot.

sewing 101

A pair of tweezers is handy to keep by the sewing machine to pull out tiny threads caught in the machine.

FABRIC IS CREEPING

Does the bottom fabric creep away from the top fabric while sewing? Pulling and tugging will not keep the fabric together (and may break the needle). When sewing, the fabric is held in place by the presser foot, which pushes upper fabric forward at the same time the feed dogs pull the lower fabric backwards. Some fabrics *creep* during this process, resulting in one piece of fabric that's longer than the other.

To prevent creeping:

- Stitch on the grain of fabric.

- Hold fabric taut while sewing.

- Use a stiletto to push upper fabric toward the needle while sewing.

- Use a roller foot or walking foot.

To prevent creeping, use a stiletto to push upper fabric toward the needle while sewing.

FABRIC PUCKERS

- Try polyester or polyester core thread, if appropriate for the fabric, as polyester thread has a slight stretch.

- The thread may be too heavy for the fabric type. Try a finer thread.

- Use the same size thread for both the needle and the bobbin.

- Needle may be bent or the point is blunt. Replace with a new needle.

- Presser foot may be too light on the fabric. Increase pressure. For machines without pressure regulators, adjust with the stitch tension.

- Upper tension may be incorrect. Test with a 6" (15cm) swatch of fabric and adjust (see page 44).

- Try a shorter stitch, such as twelve to fifteen stitches per inch.

- Lightweight fabrics pucker most when stitched on the lengthwise grain. Hold fabric firmly in the back and front of the needle while sewing.

- Fabric may not be feeding properly. Place a piece of pattern tissue or wax paper between fabric and the feed dogs.

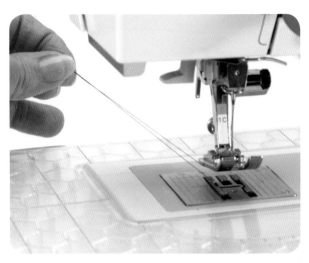

Pull threads to the rear when starting to sew, eliminating tangling and bunching on the bottom of the fabric.

Place a piece of pattern tissue or wax paper between fabric and the feed dogs to help fabric feed properly.

MACHINE JAMS OR DOES NOT FEED FABRIC

- Lint may have accumulated in bobbin area. Clean out threads and lint under needle plate, in bobbin area and bobbin case. Clean lint from feed dogs. There could even be a broken needle part in the path.

- Hold threads at the rear when starting to sew. This keeps the first stitches clean and eliminates tangling.

- The stitch length may be set at zero. Select the proper stitch length.

- Presser foot pressure may be set too low. Increase the pressure.

- Feed dogs may be lowered. Raise the feed dogs.

TUNNELED STITCHES ON LIGHTWEIGHT FABRICS

- Narrow the stitch width.

- Add appropriate stabilizer to the back of the fabric.

THREAD BUNCHES

- Feed dogs may be down. Raise the feed dogs.

- Threads may be bunched under the presser foot when starting to sew. Hold threads to the back.

- Bobbin area may have tangled threads. Remove the needle plate and clean.

- Check the needle threading path.

MACHINE JAMS/KNOCKING NOISE

- Presser foot may be loose. Tighten.

- You may be pulling on the fabric while sewing. Don't pull, just guide gently.

- Dust may have accumulated in the feed dogs. Remove needle plate and clean.

- Lint may be in the hook (if your machine has a hook). Remove the hook, clean it thoroughly and oil it.

- Threads may be bunched under the presser foot when starting to sew. Hold threads to the back.

- Needle may be bent or dull. Replace the needle.

- Machine may need to be oiled. Follow machine manual for oiling spots.

MACHINE STOPS SUDDENLY WHILE SEWING

- Machine may have been running at a low speed for an extended time. To prevent overheating, some machines will turn off automatically. If not, turn the machine off for about twenty minutes and then turn it back on.

NEEDLE WILL NOT MOVE

- Presser foot may be up. Put presser foot down.

- Thread may have run out. Replace empty spool and rethread.

- Thread may be tangled in bobbin area. Clean out.

- Buttonhole lever may be engaged. Disengage.

- Bobbin fly wheel may be engaged. Disengage.

sewing 101

Thread entanglements happen on the opposite side of the fabric from the origin of the problem. If you have a tangled nest of thread on the bottom of the fabric, the problem will be along the needle threading path.

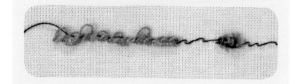

STITCHES ARE NOT FORMING PROPERLY

- Bobbin case may not be threaded properly. Rethread properly.

- Spool cap may be the wrong size for thread spool. Replace with the proper size.

- Thread may not be properly pulled into tension or thread sensor guide. Rethread.

- Needle may be bent. Replace with a new needle.

- Poor quality buttonhole stitches: Stabilize the fabric, position the buttonhole lengthwise on the fabric grain and use the proper buttonhole foot.

- Poor quality decorative stitch: Use the correct presser foot for the stitch and stabilize the fabric.

- Poor quality straight stitch: Increase stitch length and check tension setting.

MACHINE IS UNTHREADING

- Raise take-up lever before sewing.

- Cut thread ends at least six inches at the end of each seam. Pull thread tails behind and under the presser foot.

- Gently hold the threads to the back when beginning to sew.

- Ensure needle is set properly.

increasing your sphere of influence

Today's sewing machines offer a huge assortment of utilitarian and decorative stitch patterns built into the machine. Whether your machine has five stitch patterns or more than four hundred, you will certainly be anxious to experiment with them all. After all, embellishing fabrics uses our creative and fun side! Stitch functions such as utility, decorative, heirloom or quilting will enhance each and every project.

Before jumping straight to the fun part, a little initial preparation will create the perfect foundation for your sewing project. Achieving professional results depends on many "behind-the-scenes" tasks, such as proper preparation of fabric and selecting the perfect stitch length and width.

Although it is tempting to skip these "boring" preparation tasks, they are the linchpin to successful results.

3

project preparation

You have chosen your fabric and pattern and you are eager to begin sewing! There's still a lot more prep work to be done before heading to the sewing machine. Although seemingly boring, make sure you have all the tools and notions ready and your fabric properly prepared. Choose the proper pattern layout, mark accordingly and cut accurately.

sew for precision

Fabric preparation is key to achieving professional results. Haphazardly cutting the fabric or guessing at seam allowances can lead to sewing errors and disappointments. Two essential first steps are prewashing and finding the grain of fabric. Selecting the fabric and beginning to embellish the project are certainly the most enjoyable parts of sewing, but don't be tempted to skip fabric and interfacing preparation. If you do, you may have a shrunken, twisted garment after the first washing.

Noting fabric type and reading pattern instructions for proper layout are also beneficial. Some fabrics, such as silks and knits, may require additional pattern layout techniques, and plaid fabrics will need to be matched before cutting. Preparing the fabric, accurately laying out the pattern, and precisely cutting, pinning and marking pattern notches lay the foundation for a successful project.

PREWASHING MATERIALS

Before buying fabric, check the end of the bolt for fiber content and shrinkage. If you plan to wash and dry the finished project, you should wash and dry the fabric before checking for grain and cutting. Prewashing the fabric allows for shrinkage, relaxes the fabric and removes the sizing (manufacturer's finish). The resinlike sizing can quickly dull and gum up machine needles; removing it before sewing eliminates skipped stitches, puckering and dull needles.

Prewashing also removes excess dye from the fabric, helping to avoid color bleeding from one fabric onto another. If using interfacing, it must also be preshrunk to avoid puckering and warping in the finished project (see page 41). If the garment will be dry-cleaned, there's no need to prewash—the fabric is ready to test for straight of grain.

Wash, dry and iron the fabric as you would the finished garment. Before you spend time cutting and sewing, you want to see how the fabric washes. If the fabric warps during washing, it's better to find out now than after you've spent time making an entire garment.

Prewashing fabric for craft projects that aren't wearable is a personal choice. I don't prewash cottons for a quilt when I want the finished quilt to have more loft and texture.

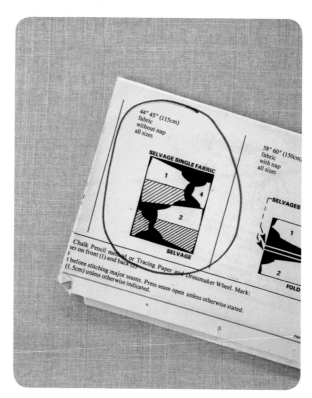

Read pattern instructions from start to finish before laying out your fabric. Always choose the pattern layout according to fabric type.

STRAIGHT OF GRAIN

Each pattern piece has a grain marking that is placed parallel to the selvage edge of the fabric. This marking must be in proper alignment with the lengthwise straight of grain and perpendicular to the crosswise grain. Failing to properly align the straight of grain can result in a poorly assembled garment. For a craft project that will not be worn, cutting on the straight of grain may not be crucial. If your pattern is to be cut on the bias, the grain marking will still be parallel to the selvage.

Check the crosswise grain to determine grain of fabric. Fold the fabric in half lengthwise. The selvage on the top layer should align perfectly with the selvage on the bottom layer, and the corners should be at right angles. The fabric should be flat and even, not bunching in any areas. If not flat, your fabric is off-grain and needs to be straightened.

Find the straight of grain by pulling a thread.

STRAIGHTENING THE GRAIN

First, find straight of grain by pulling one thread across the fabric width. Snip through the selvage, find one crosswise thread and pull. The fabric will gather until you reach the opposite side. Loosely woven fabric is easier to pull one thread all the way across. For tightly woven fabrics, pull the thread every few inches, or until it puckers. Slide the fabric along the thread until you come to the opposite selvage. Carefully cut along the pulled thread.

If the selvage has been removed, determine crosswise grain by pulling the fabric. The crosswise grain has more stretch than lengthwise grain. Hold fabric along one grainline with your hands about 1" (3cm) apart, and pull. Repeat in the other direction. The grain that has the most stretch is the crosswise grain.

Fold the fabric in half lengthwise, aligning selvages. The fabric is on-grain when corners form right angles and selvages match. If the fabric is still off-grain, repeat the process.

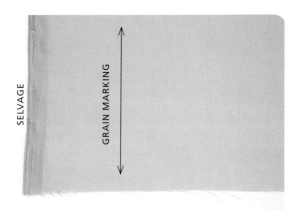

SELVAGE

GRAIN MARKING

Place the grain marking parallel with the selvage edge.

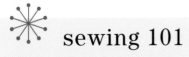

sewing 101

Don't use a design line in the fabric to determine straight of grain. The print may not match up with straight of grain. Carefully inspect print fabrics before purchasing, and avoid those that are extremely off-grain.

sewing 101

To find the grain of knits, find a crosswise loop and hand baste (using a contrasting color thread) along the grain. This provides a straight edge for folding the fabric and laying out the pattern.

PREPARE THE PATTERN

Once your fabric is on the straight of grain, the grain of the fabric will match the grainline on the pattern. Fold the fabric in half lengthwise with wrong-sides-out, matching selvage edges; this makes pinning, cutting and marking easier. If the fabric is expensive, slippery or thick, don't fold the fabric—lay it out in a single layer.

Place all pattern pieces in the same direction with right-side-up; this eliminates having two left-front pieces after cutting. If the fabric looks the same on both sides, choose one side and mark the back with chalk (see page 33). Check everything twice and cut once!

Lay out the pattern so the grainline is perfectly parallel to the selvage. Carefully measure the distance from the selvage or fold to the grainline for accuracy.

Although the fabric now has perfect straight of grain, remember that puckering may still occur when sewing woven fabrics in the lengthwise direction. Don't try to avoid this by altering the pattern layout or the garment will be distorted— always follow the manufacturer's layout instructions. Remember that when stitching lengthwise seams, loosen the upper tension on your machine and hold the fabric taut in front of and behind the needle while sewing (see page 34).

Fold the fabric in half and match the selvages.

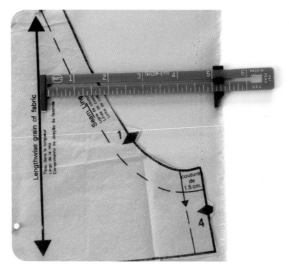

Measure the distance from the selvage to the grainline for accuracy in placement.

PATTERN LAYOUT

Most patterns have more than one layout possibility. If the fabric has a nap, directional design or a plaid to be matched, follow the pattern instructions for a napped layout. Often, this pattern is cut from a single layer, rather than two layers. Taking the extra step to match designs and plaids results in a garment that appears tailor-made. Make duplicates of each pattern piece to be cut. Mark an X on the front side of each piece to avoid cutting errors. Lay each pattern piece right-side-up facing in the correct direction.

HINTS AND TIPS:

- When working with slippery fabrics, place pattern tracing material on a flat, level surface. Place the fabric right-side-up on top of the tracing material. Lastly, place the pattern on the fabric. The tracing material prevents the fabric from slipping while cutting.

- Take the time to cut the notches shown on the pattern. Cut a single clip—not a V-shaped notch—to prevent weakening the fabric.

- Mark darts and any other markings before removing the pattern pieces. If it's hard to distinguish the right side of the fabric, make an X on the wrong side of each piece with fabric chalk.

- Use sharp shears for cutting fabric. Always keep shears on the surface while cutting. Invest in a good pair of shears and they will last a lifetime.

- Always pin pattern pieces together before sewing to keep them from shifting while stitching. Invest in good quality pins and toss out those bent ones!

- Remove pins as you stitch or be sure they're placed exactly perpendicular to the seam for less needle breakage.

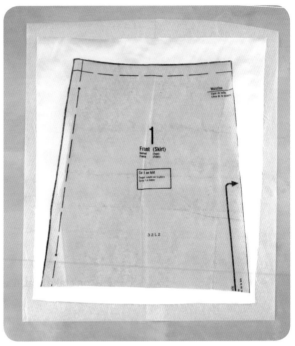

Place slippery fabric on top of pattern tracing material before cutting out the pattern.

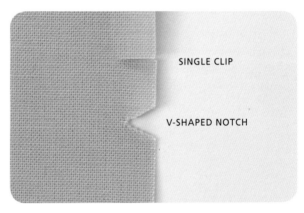

SINGLE CLIP

V-SHAPED NOTCH

Use a single notch to mark your pattern, not a V-shaped notch.

 sewing 101

Try cutting the pattern on the bias. Sheer fabrics drape wonderfully and will be ravel free.

PRESSING

Pressing will be a large component of your sewing time. Pressing as you sew keeps seams crisp and sharp, and goes a long way toward achieving fabulous results. Keep that iron handy! Press the pattern pieces before you sew, and press every seam line while sewing.

Be aware that pressing and ironing are very different. To press, place the iron on the fabric, lift up and press down at intervals. Conversely, ironing is moving the iron back and forth on the fabric; it is much rougher and stretches out the fabric, so avoid ironing.

Always test fabric scraps before pressing your pattern pieces—various fabrics respond differently to heat and steam. Be sure scorching or shiny marks are not left on the fabric. If the fabric is delicate and won't take heat, use a press cloth or press the seams open with your fingers. Fabrics that cannot be directly pressed still benefit from pressing with special techniques.

sewing 101

Never press or sew over pins! Pressing over pins will leave indentations in the fabric. If you sew over pins, you run the risk of breaking your machine's needle.

sewing 101

To set pleats, use a solution of half water and half white vinegar. Spray the solution onto a press cloth. Place the cloth on the pleats and press until almost dry. Allow the fabric and press cloth to dry completely.

When pressing, first press from the wrong side until you determine how well the fabric presses, the correct heat setting, and whether you need a press cloth. After sewing, press the seams open on the wrong side of fabric. Then turn the fabric over and press the right side. This will set in your seams. Pressing properly is a critical step in sewing.

Pressing napped fabric, such as velvet, requires special handling. Don't place an iron directly onto napped fabric. Hold the iron above the fabric for a few seconds. If you must press directly onto the napped fabric, use a needle board or terry cloth towel: Lay the napped fabric on the thick towel, and press from the wrong side, using a pressing cloth if necessary.

SEAM GUIDES

Most patterns are designed with a ⅝" (15.9mm) seam allowance. Sewing these seams accurately is important—it's amazing how quickly even ¹⁄₁₆" (1.2mm) variance can change a garment or quilt block size.

Many machines have a graduated needle plate with measurements in various increments. Line up the raw edges of the fabric with the proper line on the needle plate while sewing to maintain the desired seam allowance.

You can check your seam allowance with a cloth or plastic tape measure. The width is exactly ⅝" (15.9mm) on most measures—just right for a quick seam allowance check!

Need a temporary guide? Painter's tape makes a quick guide and peels off the machine easily without leaving residue.

Check your seam allowance against the width of a cloth or plastic tape measure.

sewing 101

When sewing, keep your eyes on the seam guide and not the needle. Watching the needle results in inaccurate seam allowances.

PROPER SEAM GUIDE PLACEMENT

To properly place any seam guide on your machine, first check the pattern instructions for the recommended seam allowance. Find that measurement on a plastic or cloth tape measure. Place the tape measure under the machine needle, lowering needle onto the desired mark. Make sure the tape measure is straight, with the metal end toward the right. Place a seam guide (or painter's tape) at the right edge of the tape measure. Stitch several inches, aligning the edge of the fabric with the guide, and check the seam measurement. Adjust if necessary.

Place the tape measure under the machine needle, lowering the needle onto the desired mark.

ADJUSTABLE NEEDLE POSITION

An adjustable needle position allows you to place the needle exactly where you need it. It is always better to move the needle instead of the fabric. For example, adjust your needle position to stitch close to a zipper or raised edge while maintaining close contact of the foot with the feed dogs. Some machines have right, left and center positions, while others can have an almost limitless number of positions left and right of center in gradual increments. Some machines offer additional positions when the twin needle option is engaged. Check your owner's manual for information on how to change the needle position.

When sewing close to the fabric's edge, the best stitching is achieved when the fabric remains over both feed dogs. It is advisable to change the needle position instead of moving and lining the fabric with the needle. To prevent needle breakage, always use a zigzag needle plate whenever changing the needle position from center. Remember to raise the needle out of the fabric before adjusting its position, or you'll break your needle.

For seam allowances (or tucks) wider than approximately ½" (12.7mm), choose the center needle position and follow the markings on the needle plate or seam guide. Adjust the needle position slightly as necessary. When sewing seam allowances from ³⁄₁₆" (4.8mm) to ½" (12.7mm), use the adjustable needle position function. Place the edge of the fabric even with the right edge of the foot and adjust the needle to the correct position.

When sewing a seam that is smaller than ³⁄₁₆" (4.8mm), use an edgestitch foot (see page 54). It's designed to sew over just one feed dog, while still keeping the fabric securely under the foot.

If your machine does not have adjustable needle position function, use a foot designed to sew over one feed dog, such as an edgestitch foot.

Incorrect! Don't move your fabric to place the needle closer to the edge. The fabric is not held securely when you move the fabric in this way.

Correct! Sew close to the edge of the fabric by changing your needle position.

sewing 101

When using a straight-stitch presser foot, the needle position must always be in the center. Any other position will break the needle.

STITCH LENGTH

Older sewing instructions and machines measure stitches to the inch, while newer ones measure stitches by millimeter. (For example, 2mm is equivalent to twelve stitches per inch.) Computerized machines automatically choose optimum stitch length and width for each stitch pattern. Most sewing machines can be adjusted manually when necessary. Check the owner's manual for more information on your specific machine.

It is important to choose the stitch length appropriate for the fabric and task in order to achieve maximum durability and appearance.

- The most common stitch length used is 2mm to 2.5mm (10–12 stitches per inch).

- Vinyls, leather, imitation leather, suede and similar fabrics require a longer stitch length of 2.5mm–4mm (6–10 stitches per inch). A shorter stitch length may cut the fabric and hinder appearance.

- A basting stitch is at least 4mm (6 stitches per inch); some machines go as high as 9mm.

- A shorter stitch length of 1.25mm (20 stitches per inch) is necessary for reinforcing certain areas, like curved seams.

- A longer stitch length is appropriate for denim and heavy fabrics, whereas a shorter stitch length is appropriate for delicate fabrics like batiste.

- Along with fabric type, think of the thread you are using when adjusting the stitch length. For example, a longer stitch is more appropriate when using heavier thread for topstitching.

sewing 101

When selecting any decorative stitch pattern, always test it first on fabric scraps. Adjusting the stitch length can dramatically change the appearance of the stitch, either distorting or improving it.

For example, lengthening the stitch on the honeycomb stitch will open it up. Shortening the stitch will cause the design to overlap. Neither may be desirable for your finished project. Always test first, and then sew!

PROPER   OPENED UP   OVERLAPPED

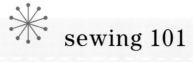

sewing 101

Proper stitch width, length and presser foot pressure are key for accurate stitches. Keep your journal handy and refer to your notes often. Find a new technique? Jot stitch length, width, needle type and fabric specifics down for later reference.

STITCH WIDTH

Stitch width is adjusted according to the stitch pattern selected. Computerized machines automatically choose optimum stitch length and width for each stitch pattern. Select a width no wider than necessary. Wide stitch widths have a tendency to tunnel (pulling in from both sides of the seam line forming a ridge), especially on lightweight fabrics. If the stitch width cannot be adjusted, try adding stabilizer to reduce tunneling.

Many machines can be adjusted from 0mm–9mm. Check your owner's manual to determine your machine's available range. A narrow stitch width is 1mm, medium is set at 2mm–3mm, and a wide stitch is 4mm or more. When adjusting the stitch width, always check that the needle clears the hole in the needle plate.

When using specialty needles, such as twin or hem-stitch needles, it is very important to carefully lower the needle by hand to ensure clearance when adjusting the stitch width. A stitch width that works for a single needle may not work for twin, triple or wing needles. Many machines have a twin needle function that limits the stitch width when using a specialty needle, but careful checking will ensure that a specialty needle isn't broken with the first stitch.

PRESSER FOOT PRESSURE

Pressure adjustment sets the amount of pressure exerted by the foot on the fabric while sewing. When setting presser foot pressure, balance is key. The correct amount of pressure keeps the fabric secure while still allowing smooth movement over feed dogs, producing a perfect stitch.

Too much pressure causes the lower fabric to move quicker than the top fabric, resulting in creeping and puckered seams. Too much pressure may also leave imprints on the fabric. Too little pressure makes it impossible to sew a straight seam line. Sometimes incorrect pressure is the result of using the wrong presser foot, which can cause fabrics to creep. Always choose the best presser foot for the task. Although newer machines automatically set presser foot pressure, manual adjustments can still be made. Learn how your machine works so proper adjustments can be made.

Each machine has the pressure regulator in different spots. Some may be on top, some on the side and others in the back. Check your manual for your machine's position.

Standard pressure is used for normal sewing work. Increase the pressure for firmer fabrics; reduce the pressure for looser knits or jerseys. This prevents the fabric from puckering, and helps the fabric feed correctly.

4

hems and edgings

Hems can be utilitarian or make a statement! Whether you choose an invisible hem or a decorative hem, stitch appearance is important. With any hem type, choose the hem that complements your fabric and project.

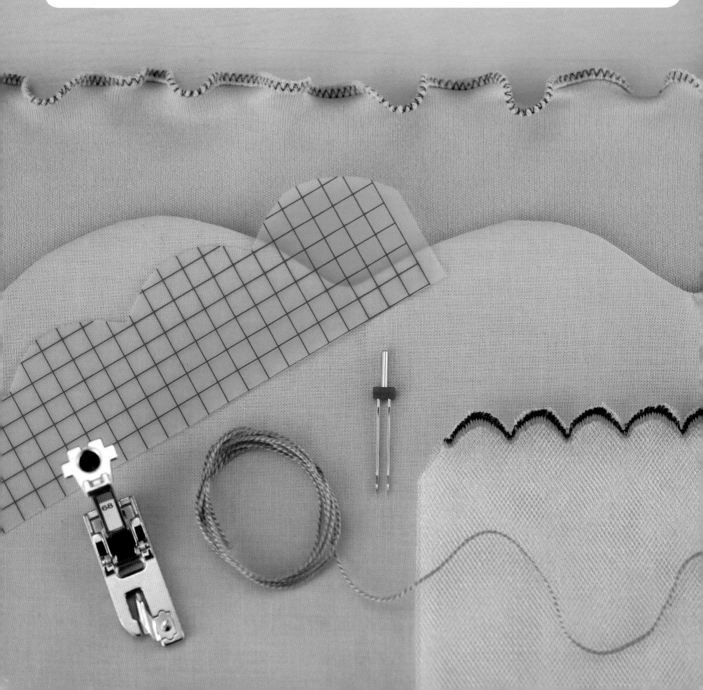

USING A HEMMER FOOT

A hemmer foot has a round channel under the foot that holds the rolled fabric securely until it reaches the needle. On the rolled hemmer foot, the channel continues to the back so the rolled hem flows smoothly under the foot. Although not every type of hem requires the use of a hemmer foot, many do. Getting the hem started with any hemmer foot is crucial to achieving a perfect hem from beginning to end. Here are two different methods for getting started with a hemmer foot—choose the one that works best for you.

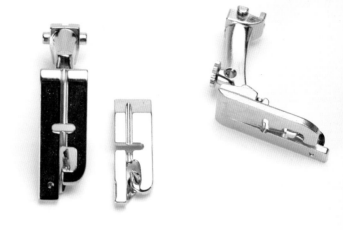

Hemmer feet

Method 1

Fold under the edge just like the hem will be rolled; finger press about 1" (2.5cm) in place. Place the folded fabric under the foot without inserting it into the scroll. Stitch ½"–¾" (12.7mm–19.1mm). While holding the back threads with one hand, raise the foot and wiggle the folded fabric into the scroll and pull the fabric forward. When inserted correctly, the folded fabric will be in the scroll, and the fabric in front of the foot will begin to fold, forming the hem. Lower the foot and begin sewing. Keep the scroll filled with a sufficient amount of fabric by gently holding the fabric in front of the foot to the left.

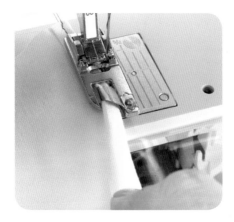

Method 1: Hold the fabric in front of the foot to the left.

Method 2

Cut a 2" (5cm)wide strip of water-soluble stabilizer the length of the hem. With the stabilizer on top, match the edge of the stabilizer and the fabric. Twirl the stabilizer and fabric into the scroll and begin sewing. The use of stabilizer provides a necessary stiffness to help guide the fabric edge into the scroll. The raw edge is completely enclosed so there isn't opportunity for fraying. When the hem is complete, cut away excess stabilizer and rinse until it's completely gone.

Method 2: Twirl the stabilizer into the scroll and begin sewing.

BLIND HEM

A blind hem is an invisible hem that is not seen on the right side of the garment. It is easily produced using the blind hem stitch pattern on the machine in conjunction with a blindstitch foot.

The blindstitch foot takes the drudgery out of hand hemming. It works with the fold of the fabric, the machine's built-in blindstitch pattern and the adjustable needle position to form even and invisible hems. The metal blade along the side keeps the fabric fold an even distance from the stitches, allowing the needle to barely penetrate the fold with a tiny stitch. The blade protrudes over the toe of the foot and through the needle opening, forcing stitches to be made over it; this keeps stitches loose and avoids puckers.

For a perfect invisible hem, adjust the amount of *bite* of each stitch by adjusting the needle position or stitch width. If adjustable needle position is unavailable, use an adjustable blindstitch foot and reposition the foot

BLIND HEM SETTINGS

Foot: Blindstitch

Needle: Universal

Stitch: Blindstitch

Stitch length: Adjust according to fabric type

Stitch width: 2.5mm (adjust as necessary)

Note: *Needle should be in far right position (adjust as necessary).*

for proper placement along the folded fabric. Use an appropriate stitch length for the fabric being sewn so the thread forms a loose stitch over the blade. Test on fabric scraps and adjust accordingly before sewing.

To produce a nearly invisible hem, use nylon monofilament thread in the needle, and 70 or 80 size needle. When using regular thread, use a needle one size smaller than normal for the fabric (see page 145).

To sew a blind hem, first serge, overcast or zigzag the raw edge. Fold the desired hem, and pin or baste it in place. Fold the garment back over the right side of the fabric. You are exposing the finished raw edge by at least ¼" (6.4mm). Place the fabric under the blindstitch foot, positioning the metal guide along the folded back edge of the fabric, and sew using the blind hem stitch. The needle should just pierce the edge of the fold. Guide the folded edge evenly along the guide of the blindstitch foot.

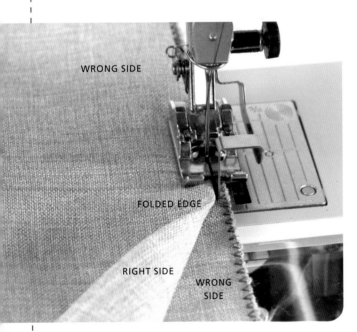

WRONG SIDE

FOLDED EDGE

RIGHT SIDE

WRONG SIDE

The needle should just pierce the edge of the fold. Guide the folded edge evenly along the center metal guide of the blindstitch foot.

sewing 101

If you quilt extensively, consider purchasing a second adjustable blindstitch foot for piecing seams. Adjust it for ¼" (6.4mm) seam. Place a drop of glue on the adjusting screw to permanently hold the guide in place.

SHELL HEM

Use a shell hemmer foot to form tiny scallops, often called a picot edge, when hemming lightweight to medium-weight fabrics. The shell hemmer foot appears similar to the rolled hemmer foot, but has a rounded and deeper groove underneath. Two sizes are available: ⅛" (3.2mm) and ¼" (6.4mm). Use this foot in conjunction with zigzag, blindstitch or overlock stitches.

The shell hem is achieved by tightening the tension so that, as it zigzags, the needle and thread draw in the fabric to create a lightly scalloped edge. Fabric such as nylon tricot gives the most distinct shells, while other fabrics produce a fainter shell hem. Increasing the stitch length increases the size of the shells. Practice on a scrap piece of similar fabric until the tension and scalloped edge are correct. Adjust tension according to fabric weight. If the zigzag stitch does not draw in to form a shell/scallop, tighten slightly. (Typically, you will need to increase upper tension to 6–8.)

Be sure to add a stitch sample and machine specifics to your journal for later reference!

SHELL HEM SETTINGS

Foot: Shell hemmer

Needle: Appropriate for fabric type

Stitch: Zigzag, blindstitch or overlock

> **Zigzag:** Stitch width 2mm–5mm

> **Blindstitch:** Stitch width 4mm, engage right/left mirror image function

> **Overlock:** Stitch width 4mm

Stitch length: 1.5mm–3mm

Note: *A longer stitch length will result in longer shells.*

Note: *Hemming corners may require changing the stitch length to 1.5mm–2.5mm.*

sewing 101

Spray starch should be in every sewing room! Use plenty of spray starch and press the folded fabric edge before hemming, especially on very lightweight fabrics.

Shell hemmer foot

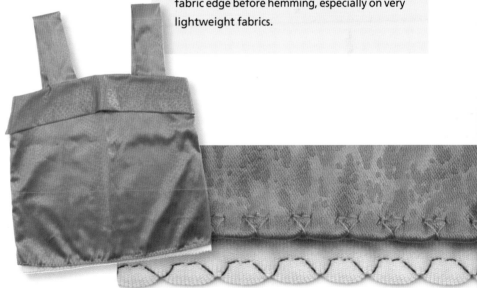

A finished shell hem on a lightweight, sheer fabric.

ROLLED AND WHIPPED HEMS

Use a rolled hemmer foot to achieve professional and very dainty hems. Rolled hems are softer and work perfectly on lightweight fabrics, as a finish for ruffles or as a narrow hem on lingerie.

Use a universal needle and a zigzag stitch. Loosen top tension if necessary. Press the first 4" (10cm) of the hem (the foot will continue to fold as it sews). Adjust the needle position so the left swing of the needle falls in the fabric past the hem and encloses it, and the right swing falls off the right edge. The fabric rolls into a tiny hemmed edge as the needle swings left. The hem has a "sawtooth" effect.

ROLLED AND WHIPPED HEM SETTINGS

Foot: Rolled hemmer

Needle: Universal appropriate for fabric

Stitch: Zigzag

Stitch length: 1.5mm

Stitch width: 3.4mm–4.5mm

Note: *Needle should be in the left position.*

The needle should fall into the fabric and then off the right edge.

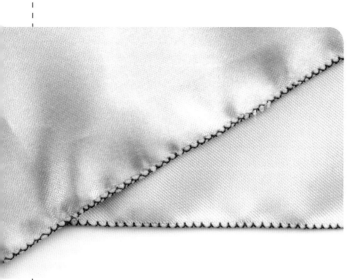

Finished rolled hem

sewing 101

Pressing the entire hem before sewing is a personal choice. For many hems I press at least the first 4" (10.2cm). While carefully sewing, I fold as I sew, stopping periodically to ensure the measurements remain consistent.

The fabric rolls into a tiny hemmed edge as the needle swings left.

TWIN NEEDLE HEM

Using twin needles to sew a hem creates perfectly parallel stitched lines and a unique topstitched appearance. The space between the lines is determined by the size of the twin needle. For example, a 4.0/80 size twin needle creates lines that are 4mm apart. Knit fabrics are perfect candidates for twin needle hems because the fabric is less bulky and a smooth hem is achieved.

To sew a twin needle hem, first serge, overcast or zigzag the raw edge. Use a zigzag or open-toe foot, and engage the twin needle function on your machine. If this function isn't available, handcrank the needles through the first stitch to ensure the needles won't hit the foot.

Place a strip of water-soluble stabilizer on top of the fabric to prevent wavy stitches. For a perfect parallel topstitched hem, measure the depth of the hem and add an additional ¼" (6.4mm) to ensure the raw edge will be caught in the stitching. Fold up the hem and stitch from the top side of the fabric to achieve a hem like those on T-shirts. Trim excess fabric from the back close to the stitching line to finish. Rinse away excess stabilizer.

TWIN NEEDLE HEM SETTINGS

Foot: Zigzag or open-toe

Needle: Twin appropriate for fabric

Stitch: Straight or decorative

Stitch length: Adjust according to fabric type

Stitch width: Adjust according to fabric type

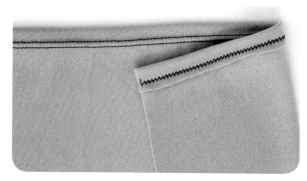

Fold the hem toward the the wrong side of the fabric and stitch from the top.

WIRED HEM

Sewing a wired hem adds body without weight, creating billowy hems on stretchy or bias-cut fabric. The edge is stiffened by inserting stiff plastic, fishing line or wire into the fold of the narrow hem.

Fold fishing line or wire inside the hem.

WIRED HEM SETTINGS

Foot: Embroidery, zigzag, hemmer or open-toe

Needle: Universal appropriate for fabric

Stitch: Satin

Stitch length: 0.5mm–1mm

Stitch width: 3.5–5mm

Use an embroidery, zigzag, hemmer or open-toe foot, and a satin stitch (width 3.5–5mm, length 0.5mm–1mm). Press a narrow hem. Place wire in the hem fold. Stitch as for a lettuce hem (see page 78), pulling gently in front of and behind the presser foot.

LETTUCE HEM

The lettuce hem adds a natural frill to hems and edges that stretch, or are hemmed on the bias. For the perfect lettuce look, take advantage of the *curl* of the fabric. Hold a fabric edge in each hand and pull slightly apart. The fabric will curl to the wrong side of the fabric; this is the direction you should fold your hem.

For a folded hem, turn the fabric over ⅛" (3.2mm) two times, and press. For a single-fold hem, turn over ⅛" (3.2mm) and press. Using a satin stitch, sew slowly and fold the fabric as you go. Adjust the needle position so the needle falls off the fold on the right-hand swing of each stitch. Hold the fabric in front of and behind the foot, stretching gently while sewing. The more you stretch, the greater lettuce effect you achieve.

LETTUCE HEM SETTINGS

Foot: Open-toe, embroidery or zigzag

Needle: Universal or stretch appropriate for fabric

Stitch: Satin

Stitch length: 0.5mm–1mm

Stitch width: 3.5–5mm

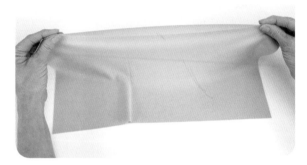

Find the curl of the fabric by pulling in opposite directions along one edge. The curl rolls to the wrong side of the fabric.

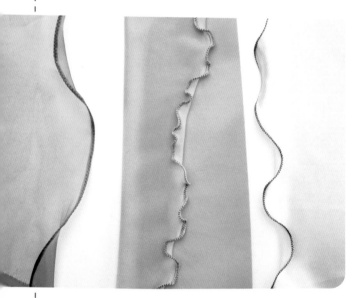

Finished lettuce hems with varying degrees of lettuce effect.

Hold the fabric in front of and behind the foot, stretching gently while sewing.

JEAN HEM

Achieving perfect hems on heavyweight fabrics requires as little bulk as possible. Serge or overcast the raw edges, and turn up once to hem. For the traditional look of hemmed jeans, use a large topstitching needle and heavy topstitching or jeans thread. Select needle size 100 or 110 when using jeans thread. Increase the stitch length.

If the hem is bulky at seams, use a *shim* to achieve even stitches. When the presser foot begins to angle upward over the hem, stop with the needle down in the fabric. Raise the presser foot, and place a shim under the back of the foot to raise it to the height of the seam. Continue sewing until the foot begins to fall off the thickness. Raise the fabric in the back of the foot gently with your hand and continue sewing. This allows the foot to slide off the thick seam onto the thinner area without skipping stitches. Another option is to remove the shim from behind the presser foot after the foot clears it, and place it in front of the foot. When the back of the foot clears the shim, remove it and continue sewing.

sewing 101

- A Jean-a-ma-jig (from Dritz) is a commercial plastic shim. Check for a specific foot or shim for your machine. You can also use folded cardboard or thick plastic as a makeshift shim.

- Decorative edgings will embellish any edge, turning a ho-hum garment into something unique. When you want a more-than-ordinary hem, take advantage of decorative stitches and special needles.

JEAN HEM SETTINGS

Foot: Straight-stitch, jeans or zigzag

Needle: Large topstitching appropriate for fabric and thread

Stitch: Straight

Stitch length: 2.5mm–4mm

Stitch width: 0mm

Note: *Needle should be in center position.*

Use a shim to raise the presser foot to the height of the seam.

SCALLOPED EDGE HEM

The scallop stitch forms a continuous wave and is an easy and elegant alternative to a straight stitch hem on blouse collars, dresses and around necklines or pants. Additional fabric may need to be added to the hem length as a scalloped hem uses more fabric than a straight hem—measure carefully before cutting.

Fabric choice is important so the apex of the scallop is clearly shown. This hem requires extensive and meticulous cutting, so don't choose fabrics that fray badly. Firmly woven fabrics such as cotton, linen and firmly woven dupioni silk are good choices. Stay away from loosely woven fabrics and fabrics with extensive bulk. Serge, zigzag or overcast the raw edge.

To make the scallop, use a zigzag or embroidery foot. A foot with high visibility is best. Select the scallop stitch on your machine. Adjust the stitch width for a longer or shorter scallop.

Adjust a single layer hem to accommodate the height of your scallop and press in place. You will be stitching on the wrong side of the fabric, about 1" (2.5cm) from the fabric edge (not directly on the edge). Position the presser foot so the inward stitches fall just below the overcast edge and begin sewing.

When completed, trim near the stitches being sure to not cut into them. Sharp scissors are a must when cutting the finished scallops. When cutting, cut from the curve toward the apex. The smaller the scallops, the more time this task will take. Take your time! The results are worth it. If necessary, use a seam sealant to secure the cut edges.

SCALLOPED EDGE HEM SETTINGS

Foot: Zigzag or embroidery

Needle: Universal appropriate for fabric

Stitch: Scallop

Stitch length: 0.5mm

Stitch width: As desired for scallop length

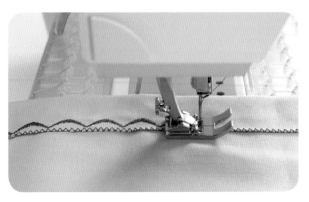

Position the presser foot so the inward stitches fall just below the overcast edge.

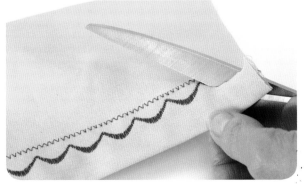

Trim near the stitches being sure to not cut into them.

sewing 101

If sewing scallops on fabrics such as tulle, don't fold the fabric; sew the scallops on a single layer of fabric. If necessary, add water-soluble stabilizer underneath the tulle.

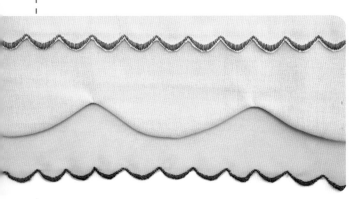

Scallops are a beautiful finish for hems, necklines or even blouse fronts.

Using a Scalloped Template

If a scallop stitch isn't available on your machine, make a scalloped-edge template. Fold up and pin a single-layer hem. Place the template on the edge of the fabric ensuring the hem depth accommodates the scallop. Trace the scallops around the entire hem. Select a satin stitch and slowly stitch along the traced line. Trim as described on page 80. Stitches will be visible.

A second method creates a *facing*. Serge, overcast or zigzag the raw edges. With right sides together, fold up a hem, ensuring the hem depth accommodates the scallops. Trace and stitch the design using a straight stitch. Trim close to the sewn edge, clipping in each apex. Turn the fabric to the right side and press. Choose this method when you want a clean appearance.

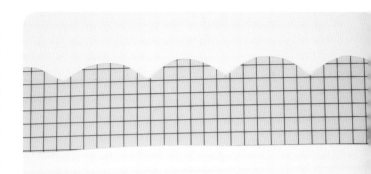

If the scallop stitch isn't available on your machine, make your own scalloped-edge template.

CORDED SCALLOP

The corded scallop simulates hand crochet with the stitches falling off the edge of the fabric. They can be added to the edge of the hem, or they can be sewn off the edge.

Use fine cording such as pearl cotton to stabilize the scallop. Use an embroidery, edgestitch, open-toe or zigzag foot for best visibilty while stitching. Place heavy water-soluble stabilizer under the edge.

Use a scallop stitch with stitch width 4mm–5mm and a satin stitch length. Slightly loosen the upper tension. Place stabilizer under the fabric and position the fabric under the foot so the point of the scallop just catches the fabric edge. Adjust the needle position as necessary. If needle position adjustment is not an option, half the foot will be on and half will be off the fabric.

If you are using a cording foot, place cording directly under the foot or through the small hole. Leave a thread tail about 2" (5cm) long behind the foot. Hold the cording with your right hand and begin sewing. Guide the fabric with the other hand. Cording becomes encased within the stitches. Carefully remove stabilizer when finished.

CORDED SCALLOP SETTINGS

Foot: Embroidery, edgestitch, open-toe or zigzag

Needle: Universal appropriate for fabric

Stitch: Scallop

Stitch length: 0.5mm

Stitch width: 4mm–5mm

Hold cording with right hand, and begin sewing. Guide the fabric with the other hand.

SCALLOP-OFF-THE-EDGE

Add multiple rows of scallops to the edge for a lacy, crocheted effect. Sew as for corded scallops (see page 81). Place water-soluble stabilizer under the edge and extending 2" (5.1cm) past the edge. Align the center of the foot with the fabric edge and sew. Add additional rows as desired, alternating the fall of the scallops. Each additional row will connect to the previous one in the middle of the extended scallop. Sew slowly and make sure the second scallop connects sufficiently with the previous one. Trim excess stabilizer and rinse completely in warm water to remove remaining stabilizer. Practice with a variety of thread weights.

sewing 101

To avoid bits of frayed fabric showing through the scallop, use several layers of water-soluble stabilizer. You can also use construction paper that matches the thread in place of the stabilizer.

SCALLOP-OFF-THE-EDGE SETTINGS

Foot: Embroidery, edgestitch, open-toe or zigzag

Needle: Universal appropriate for fabric

Stitch: Scallop

Stitch length: 0.5mm

Stitch width: 4mm–5mm (or as desired)

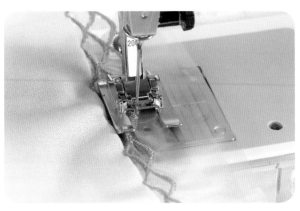

Each additional row of scallops will connect to the previous one in the middle of the extended scallop.

TWIN NEEDLE SCALLOP HEM

Use a twin needle with a scallop stitch on sheer fabrics in place of a traditional hem that would show through. If the fabric tends to fray, first finish the raw edge with a narrow zigzag stitch. Set the machine for a scallop stitch, adjust stitch width and length as desired. Press the hem allowance to the wrong side. Stitch from the right side, staying at least ¼ " (6.4mm) from the raw edge of the hem allowance. Trim excess fabric up to the stitching line on the bottom edge.

TWIN NEEDLE SCALLOP HEM SETTINGS

Foot: Zigzag (to accomodate needles)

Needle: Twin appropriate for fabric

Stitch: Scallop

Stitch length: As desired

Stitch width: As desired

Finished twin needle scallop hem on sheer fabric

CORDED DECORATIVE HEM

Make a narrow hem more decorative by using any stitch that sews side to side, such as the pin stitch. A corded hem is made by sewing pearl cotton, tatting thread or crochet thread along the folded edge. A cording foot works best for keeping the cording straight along the folded edge.

CORDED DECORATIVE HEM SETTINGS

Foot: Cording, embroidery, zigzag or open-toe

Needle: Universal appropriate for fabric

Stitch: Any side-to-side stitch

Stitch length: 0.8mm

Stitch width: 2mm–2.5mm

If using a cording foot, thread the cording through the small hole on the front of the foot. For all other feet, place the cording to the right of the fold while sewing, ensuring it is encased by the stitches. Select a side-to-side stitch, a 2mm–2.5mm stitch width, and 0.8mm stitch length to achieve a very tiny stitch. Adjust the stitch width so the right side of the stitch goes over the cord and the left side goes into fabric. Trim excess fabric up to stitching on the wrong side.

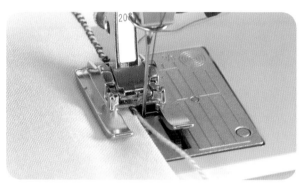

A corded hem is made by sewing pearl cotton, tatting thread or crochet thread along the folded edge.

FOLD-OVER ELASTIC BIAS TAPE

Fold-over elastic bias tape is a soft knit elastic with a fold line running along the center for easy folding. Use in place of bias tape for hems, or use on arm holes, necklines, diaper legs, bags, lingerie and blouses for a softer, gathered effect. Fold-over elastic bias tape is available in various widths from ½"–1" (12.7mm–25.4mm) in herringbone, shiny and matte finishes. The color choices are extensive!

To apply, align the raw edge of the fabric with the fold line of the elastic (don't fold the elastic in half). Using a narrow zigzag stitch, sew close to the edge of the elastic, pulling the tape gently in front of and behind the needle

FOLD-OVER ELASTIC BIAS TAPE SETTINGS

Foot: Open-toe or zigzag

Needle: Appropriate for fabric

Stitch: Zigzag

Stitch length: 0.5mm

Stitch width: Appropriate for fabric

while sewing. Fold the elastic along the fold line to the other side, covering the previous row of stitches and encasing the raw edge. Sew along the tape edge in the same way. The more you pull while sewing, the more the end result will be gathered.

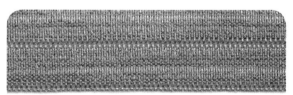

FOLD LINE

Fold-over elastic bias tape has a fold line running along the center.

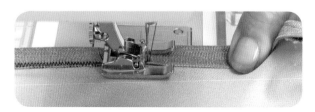

Fold the elastic along the fold line to the other side and sew along the edge.

5

buttonholes and zippers

Buttonholes and zippers are often taken for granted even though they are found throughout our wardrobes. Yet, the thought of sewing buttonholes or inserting a zipper might be so intimidating that we plan our garments without them. No more! With some fabric scraps and a little practice, you will soon be eager to add buttonholes and zippers for both utility and decoration.

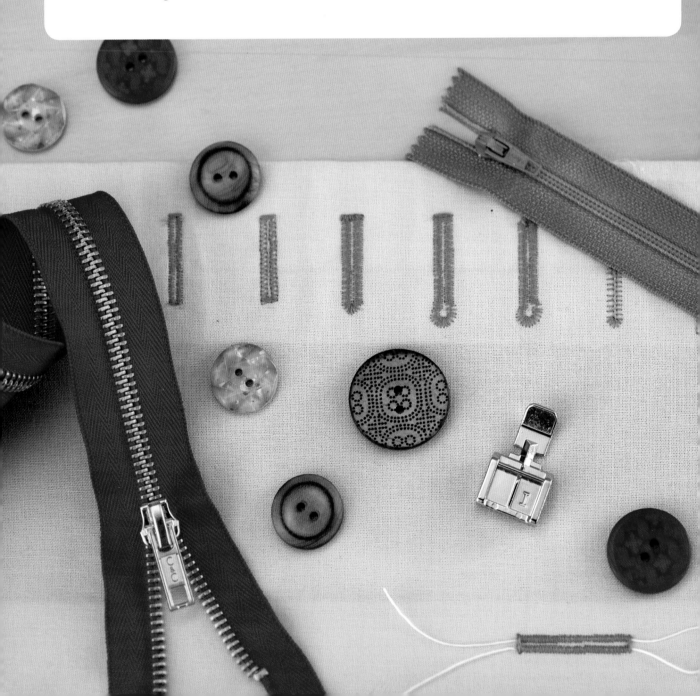

buttonholes

Buttonholes are usually "center-front," and can be merely functional or highly embellished. There are as many types and uses of buttonholes and eyelets as there are of fabrics. A standard buttonhole works for fine- to medium-weight fabrics and on blouses, shirts and pants. For heavyweight fabrics, choose a keyhole buttonhole with a normal bar tack.

BUTTONHOLE TIPS

- Stabilize and interface adequately. The finished buttonhole should be firm but not too stiff.

- If fabric is thick (and washable), place wash-away stabilizer on top of the fabric. This prevents the buttonhole from becoming lost in the fabric. Rinse away the stabilizer when finished.

- If fabric is thick (and non-washable), use a thicker thread to avoid losing the buttonhole in the fabric.

- Mark the buttonhole accurately. Place it ⅝" (15.9mm) from the garment edge. Use a commercial buttonhole guide or make your own.

- Increase upper tension to give the beads (the sides of the buttonhole) a slightly rounded and more attractive appearance.

- Use gimp to reinforce and enhance appearance (see page 121). Match the project and fabric with a complementary buttonhole style in both stability and appearance.

- Use fabric sealant to seal the buttonhole edges.

- Use horizontal buttonholes at stress points and on closely fitted garments. Vertical buttonholes are great on knit fabrics, thin bands and plackets.

- *Practice!* Always test-sew using fabric, thread, needle and stabilizer similar to that used in the finished project. Test all variables. Check the stitch length, width and tension. What interfacing works best? Should your buttonholes be placed vertically or horizontally? Try various types of thread—different weights can change the buttonhole appearance. Also match thread weight to fabric type (see chart on page 145).

- Always start with a new needle to avoid any snag lines in the fabric.

BUTTONHOLE TYPES

Choosing the proper buttonhole to match the fabric weight and project aesthetic improves both appearance and durability.

 **Standard:** Blouses, trousers, shirts. Fine- to medium-weight fabrics.

 **Heirloom (narrow):** Blouses, shirts, dresses, trousers, children's clothes, heirloom sewing. Fine- to medium-weight fabrics.

 **Stretch:** Stretch fabrics.

 **Round with normal or horizontal bar tack:** Clothing, jackets, coats. Medium- to heavyweight fabrics.

 **Keyhole:** Jackets, coats, trousers, leisure wear. Heavyweight fabrics.

 **Keyhole with tapered end:** Jackets, coats, leisure wear. Firm, non-stretchable fabric.

 **Hand-look:** Blouses, dresses, trousers, children's and baby clothes, and crafts. Fine- to medium-weight fabrics.

 **Straight stitch:** For reinforcing buttonholes and pocket edges, especially leather and imitation leather. Also can be used for welt pockets and bound buttonholes.

sewing 101

- To determine the length of the buttonhole needed, measure the button. It is generally the button width, plus the height, plus ⅛" (3.2mm). The height measurement allows extra room for ball or half-ball buttons.

- To sew consistently-sized buttonholes, use the buttonhole foot with the machine's built-in buttonhole stitch. Some machine models have a buttonhole foot with a sensor that actually detects the size and shape of the first buttonhole, and repeats for each buttonhole. The machine's quick reverse function is utilized for this. Other machines have built-in buttonhole stitches, but the buttonhole size is controlled manually using the size of the button.

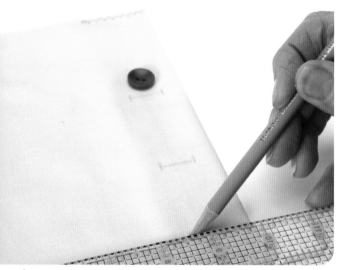

Measure and mark accurately for professional results.

MARKING BUTTONHOLES

Measure the button (as described at left) and determine placement on the garment. The first decision is whether the buttonhole should be horizontal or vertical. Tailored buttonholes are typically placed horizontally—perpendicular to the edge of the garment—for additional strength.

Next, make a small mark or insert a pin to indicate the placement for each button. Measure to make sure they are equally spaced from one another.

Using a removable marker, begin marking each buttonhole. Mark the horizontal length of each buttonhole opening, and draw short vertical marks on each end. If the buttonhole is 1" (2.5cm) long, measure ⅝" (15.9mm) in from the edge of the fabric and make a short vertical end mark. Measure 1" (2.5cm) to the left of this mark and draw a second short vertical mark. Connect these two marks with a ruler to mark the length of the buttonhole. It is helpful to extend this mark so it is easily visible while sewing.

MANUAL BUTTONHOLER

Manual buttonholers can require a two-step, four-step, five-step or six-step process depending on the machine. Check the machine manual for the exact procedure for your buttonhole foot.

The buttonhole foot has a slider and markings to guide needle placement. Attach the buttonhole foot. Place the button into the back slot and pull the slide up snugly.

Lower the machine's buttonhole lever. Select a buttonhole stitch. Don't force the buttonholer into place; it is springlike and will fall into place with a little push. Place the marked fabric under the foot and match the horizontal mark farthest from you with the red line on the buttonhole foot. Place the needle on the horizontal mark. Lower the foot and begin sewing. To keep the top thread from tangling in the buttonhole, stop after several stitches and clip excess thread.

At the next horizontal line, stop with the last stitch on the left of the zigzag and the needle out of the fabric. Following your machine's manual, adjust the stitch selector for the return stitches.

FIVE-STEP AND SIX-STEP BUTTONHOLERS

A five-step buttonholer sews the first bead forward and the second bead in reverse. Stitches on each side will always look a little different from each other, and never entirely match.

The six-step buttonholer has an additional step. The first bead is sewn forward, a straight stitch sews back to the top, and the second bead is also sewn forward. Both beads will look similar.

AUTOMATIC BUTTONHOLER WITH SENSOR

Computerized machines have a memory function for buttonholes. This allows sewing any size and type of buttonhole, each one exactly the same. Measure and mark the first buttonhole, drawing a horizontal line at the top and bottom of the buttonhole. Select the desired buttonhole stitch. Begin sewing at the top vertical line and down the first side. At the bottom vertical line, tap the machine's reverse sewing button and continue sewing.

The machine's memory will retain this buttonhole length for each consecutive button. Always let the sewing machine sew the last securing stitches. They both secure and begin the next buttonhole at the proper spot.

CUTTING BUTTONHOLES

Cut the buttonhole with a buttonhole cutter or seam ripper. Using a buttonhole cutter and block gives a nice clean cut and lessens the chance of cutting through stitching. Place the block on a stable surface and put the completed buttonhole on it. Put the blade in the center of the buttonhole and press down firmly. The cutter has beveled edges that prevent cutting through the buttonhole beads.

To cut keyhole buttonholes, a special keyhole-style cutter is available with an eyelet punch.

When using a seam ripper, carefully cut from one end of the buttonhole to the middle. Then cut from the other end to the middle. Placing pins horizontally across the end of the buttonhole, just inside the bar tack, is a precaution against slicing through the entire buttonhole.

Place the button into the back slot and pull the slide up snugly.

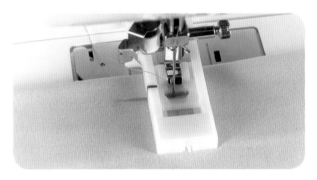

Align the horizontal mark farthest from you with the red line on the buttonhole foot.

Use a buttonhole cutter and block to cut buttonholes.

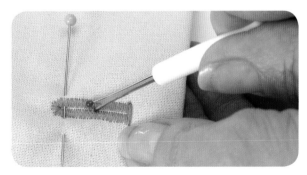

Place pins horizontally across the end of the buttonhole when opening with a seam ripper.

CORDED BUTTONHOLES

Stitching buttonholes over cording benefits heavyweight fabrics, adds stability to knits and supports areas of stress such as waistlines. Corded buttonholes give a raised, textured effect. The cording fits on hooks at the back of the buttonhole foot, runs underneath the foot and up the front, securing in the notches at the front of the foot.

Slightly reduce the upper tension. Use a fine cord, such as gimp cord, pearl cotton #8, embroidery floss, buttonhole twist, filler cord or crochet thread. Hook the cord over the spur on the back of the buttonhole foot. Pull both ends of the cord forward underneath the foot and slide each end into a slot on the front. Pull taut, making sure the cording isn't twisted.

Adjust the stitch width as necessary to stitch over the cord. Sew the buttonhole in the usual manner; the buttonhole will form over the cord, encasing it. Do not pull tightly on the cord while sewing.

When finished sewing, remove the cording from the back of the foot and remove the fabric. Pull the cord ends so the looped end is under the bartack. Draw the cords to the back of fabric with a hand sewing needle, or snip off the excess length. For knitted fabrics, pull cords to the wrong side of the fabric and tie off.

BUTTONHOLES ON STRETCH FABRICS

When sewing buttonholes on stretch fabrics, stitch over gimp thread. Follow the directions for *Corded Buttonholes*. When finished, carefully pull the gimp thread to eliminate any slack in the stitches and trim off the excess. Pull gently on one end of the gimp until the loop is drawn up to the buttonhole. With a heavy needle, pull the ends of the gimp to the back of the fabric and secure.

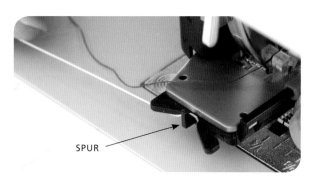

SPUR

Hook the cord over the spur at the back of the buttonhole foot.

Pull both ends of the cord forward underneath the foot and slide each end into a slot on the front.

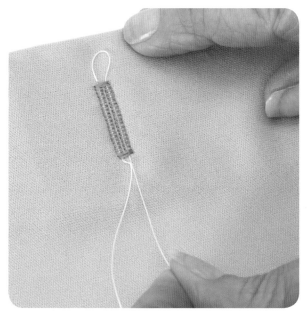

Carefully pull the gimp thread to eliminate slack in the stitches.

FRINGED BUTTONHOLES

Follow the instructions for corded buttonholes using cording, yarns, or metallic threads. When finished, snip the loop at each end to create fringe. Cut them short, leave them long, add knots—be creative!

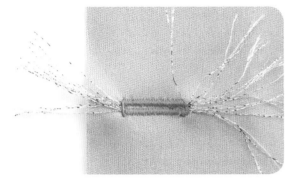

Add texture and interest to projects by using fringed buttonholes.

KEYHOLE BUTTONHOLES

Keyhole buttonholes are designed with an eyelet opening at one end to accommodate the shank of a large button on heavy fabrics, such as on a suit or heavy coat. The rounded end (keyhole) of the buttonhole is positioned at the center line so the button sits in the keyhole when fastened. Add extra strength by using buttonhole thread and cording.

After completing the keyhole buttonhole, use an eyelet punch or awl to make a hole in the rounded end of the buttonhole. Cut the rest of the buttonhole open with a buttonhole cutter or a seam ripper (see page 87).

The rounded end of a keyhole cutter

DELICATE BUTTONHOLES

Buttonhole problems are most common on lightweight, delicate fabrics. Interfacing is rarely used on sheer fabrics because it shows through. To prevent puckering, use lightweight, tear-away stabilizer underneath delicate fabrics. When finished stitching the buttonhole, carefully tear the stabilizer away. If the buttonhole needs additional strength at stress areas, sew corded buttonholes using pearl cotton, buttonhole twist or crochet thread.

Buttonholes on any delicate fabric require a finer and less dense buttonhole. Choose a narrow heirloom or hand-look buttonhole stitch pattern. Use extra fine 60 or 80 weight thread for top and bottom threads. Select a needle appropriate in type and size for fabric and thread (see chart on page 145). If puckering or tunneling occurs, reduce the upper tension for smoother stitches.

Use tear-away stabilizer and pearl cotton to create corded buttonholes on delicate fabrics.

BOUND BUTTONHOLES

Bound buttonholes add a clean professional finish to garments, especially on jackets. Generally, bound buttonholes are rectangular with each welt about ⅛" (3.2mm) wide, but the welt should be wider when using very bulky fabric. For added support, use fusible interfacing on the wrong side of the fabric.

First, determine and mark the dimensions of the rectangular buttonhole, which will be slightly longer than the button. For example, if using a ¾" (19mm) button, the buttonhole will measure approximately ⅜" (9.5mm) long and 1" (2.5cm) wide. Cut a rectangular patch of matching or contrasting fabric 2" (5cm) longer than the finished buttonhole and three times the width plus 2" (5cm).

Center the fabric rectangle over the buttonhole placement lines with right sides together. Baste in place and double check placement. With basting as your guide, machine stitch the rectangular "window" shape. Overlap stitching at beginning and ending to eliminate bulk. If sewing several buttonholes, repeat this step with all before continuing.

Draw a line lengthwise through the center of the buttonhole. Cut through both layers of fabric down the middle of the buttonhole, and then from that line diagonally out to each corner.

Turn the fabric rectangle through the center cut toward the wrong side of the fabric. Press the short ends straight to create a crisp edge. Press the seam allowance (two long sides) toward the center. Manipulate the fabric around the long edges of the opening so the welts meet in the middle. Pin next to the seam lines. You can baste the welts together to ensure they stay in place while finishing the edges. Press from the wrong side. The front is now finished, and you're ready to complete the back.

Working from the wrong side, turn under the edges of the fabric rectangle and handstitch them in place. Working from the front, add any necessary stitches to the corners to keep them square. Remove any basting stitches that kept the welt closed.

Note: The width of the welt depends on the fabric type. Delicate, thin fabric uses a small ⅛" (3.2mm) welt, while heavier fabric requires a larger ¼" (6.4mm) welt.

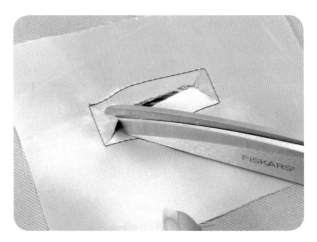

Cut through both layers of fabric down the middle and then diagonally to each corner.

Turn the fabric rectangle edges through the center cut.

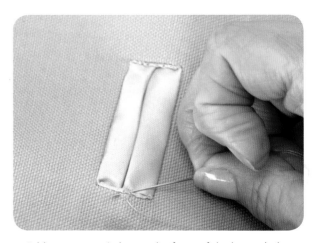

Add necessary stitches to the front of the buttonhole to keep the corners square.

BELT LOOPS

Need to sew belt loops from heavyweight fabric? Use a blindstitch pattern to sew belt loops without turning the tube. Fold a fabric strip in half lengthwise with wrong sides together. Select a 2.5mm stitch width and length, and place the needle in the center position. Sew along the raw edges with the zigzag swing of the needle on the fabric, and the straight stitch off the edge. Fold the tube so that the stitched edge is in the center of the tube. Select a straight stitch and topstitch along both edges. Change the needle position if necessary. The blindstitch allows the layers to be pulled flat after sewing.

sewing 101

The edgestitch foot can be used to maintain an even stitch close to the edge (see page 54).

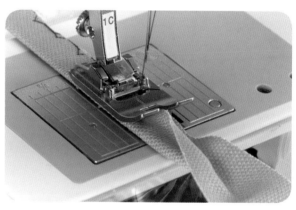

Sew along the raw edges with the zigzag swing of the needle on the fabric, and the straight stitch off the edge.

Finished buttonholes with motif embellishments

EMBELLISHED BUTTONHOLES

Adding motifs quickly embellishes traditional buttonholes. After you are finished sewing the buttonholes, remove the buttonhole foot and attach an embroidery or zigzag foot. Choose a decorative stitch, such as a flower or leaf design, and stitch the motif along the sides, above or below the buttonhole. Do several test sews to determine size and placement.

Finished belt loop

SEWING ON BUTTONS

Now that your buttonholes are perfect, you need to sew on all those buttons! Use your machine instead of tediously sewing by hand. The button sew-on foot is designed to firmly hold the button in place while the machine effortlessly sews it on using the zigzag stitch. The foot is designed to sew two-hole or four-hole flat buttons. Try using the button sew-on stitch to attach charms, ribbons or even hooks-and-eyes to fabric.

If you don't have a button sew-on foot, use a wide foot, such as the buttonholer or open-toe foot. Adjust the stitch width to allow the needle to easily enter each hole.

Get Started

Attach the button sew-on foot and select a zigzag or button sew-on stitch. If using the zigzag stitch, set the stitch length to zero and lower or cover the feed dogs. Place the fabric under the foot. Position the button on top of fabric with the left hole adjacent to the toe of the foot—regardless of the spacing in the button. Tape the button to the fabric to prevent movement, if desired. Lower the foot onto the button. Turn the handwheel to ensure the needle does not hit the button as it zigzags.

When sewing a four-hole button, sew two holes first; then raise the foot, position the foot on the second set of holes and sew again.

Shank Buttons

A button shank (a stem on the back of the button) separates the button from the attached fabric so that it can more easily pass through a buttonhole (particularly useful with heavy fabrics, like wool). A true shank button with a plastic or metal shank needs to be sewn on by hand, but you can easily add a thread shank to any flat button. To make a shank button, place a needle or toothpick in the foot's groove, extending toward the back. Take several small and straight securing stitches. Check the stitch width to make sure the needle will enter the second hole. Continue sewing slowly while the zigzag stitch moves from one hole to the next. Repeat until enough threads have formed over the needle/toothpick.

When finished, select a straight stitch and take several securing stitches in the hole. (If you have used the button sew-on stitch, the securing stitches are made automatically.) Remove the needle/toothpick and raise presser foot. Cut the threads, leaving an 8" (20cm) tail. Wind the extra thread around the thread-shank to create the shank. Tie a final knot in the thread to hold in place.

Flat Buttons

To sew a button without leaving a shank, follow the method for shank buttons, but don't place a toothpick or needle in the groove, allowing the button to be sewn flat.

Don't have a button sew-on foot? A fringe foot could be used. Select a zigzag stitch, and set the stitch length at 0. Place a button under the foot, sew six or seven stitches and raise the foot. Gently slide the stitches off the foot's center bar, leaving long tails to tie off. Pull the button gently up, separating the button and base fabric to allow the thread shank to *float* between them. Thread a hand needle with the thread tail, wrap the thread around the thread shank, pull to the back and tie off. This prevents sewing the button so close to the fabric that it won't go into the buttonhole. Apply a liquid-plastic solution, like Fray Check, to the ends if necessary.

Use the button sew-on stitch to attach charms, ribbons or even hooks-and-eyes.

zippers

Eventually you will need to insert a zipper into a garment or a tote bag. With a bit of preparation, the task will be easier and the final results will be stunning! With so many choices, which zipper to choose? Check out the notions section of any sewing shop and you'll find a rainbow of color choices. In addition to matching the zipper color to the fabric, it is important to choose the proper type to complement your project.

TYPES OF ZIPPERS

Zippers come in a variety of lengths, types and materials, so always select the best zipper type and material to improve the appearance and durability of your sewing project. Zipper teeth are manufactured from three types of materials—metal, molded plastic chain and coil (nylon). Zippers also fall into three categories—tooth, coil and invisible. Zippers can be open at one or both ends, closed at both ends or invisible.

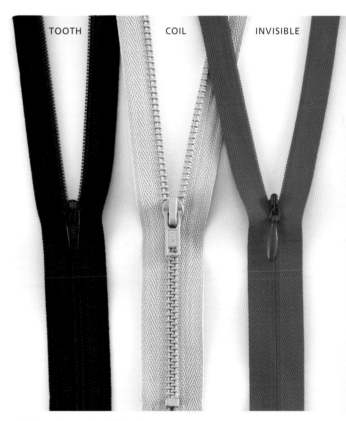

Coil, tooth and invisible zippers

- **Tooth zippers:** Teeth are equally visible on both sides of the zipper tape. Every tooth is separate. They are perfect for most straight applications like jackets, garment bags and totes.

- **Coil zippers (nylon):** Flat on one side with teeth on the other. Each tooth is connected to the next and bend easily. Use for backpacks, sleeping bags and tents. Shorter lengths can be used in purses and totes.

- **Invisible zippers:** Hidden in a seam with only the pull tab showing. They are flexible and strong. Use an invisible zipper foot to insert. Use in skirts, blouses, dresses—anywhere you need an invisible closure with a smooth finish.

 sewing 101

Invisible zippers are a type of coil zipper, but they remain in a class of their own due to their *invisibility* and special application techniques.

ZIPPER LENGTHS

How do you decide if you need a 7" (18cm) or a 9" (23cm) zipper to fit an opening? Zippers are always measured from end stops, regardless of the zipper style. It is better to select a zipper that is longer than the opening—it is much easier to shorten a zipper than to try and use one that is too small.

ZIPPER TIPS AND TRICKS

- For the least intrusive zipper, choose a nylon invisible zipper.

- The type of zipper foot used is dependent on the type of zipper. All zipper installations require the use of a zipper foot, but the invisible zipper is designed to be sewn with an invisible zipper foot.

- Metal zippers do not last as long as plastic zippers. To free a frozen metal zipper, grab a pencil—graphite is a natural lubricant. Just run the pencil tip along the teeth, and then pull the tab up and down.

- When ironing near a plastic zipper, take care to avoid melting the coils.

- Always shorten a zipper from the top if the top edge will be finished with a waistband or collar. If the top of the zipper is finished with a facing, shorten from the bottom of the zipper.

sewing 101

Before inserting a zipper into a garment, insert a 1" (2.5cm) wide strip of lightweight, fusible interfacing along the seam allowance line. This adds stability and prevents stretching, especially when sewing on lightweight or stretch fabrics.

sewing 101

Zipper tape is the woven fabric on both sides of the coils. Most have a distinct woven center line to follow while sewing.

To free a frozen metal zipper, run a pencil tip along the teeth.

- Choose the best zipper weight (gauge) to complement the project. Choose lightweight for all-purpose projects and heavyweight for backpacks, heavy bags, tents and luggage.

- Choose a zipper 2" (5cm) longer than the opening to avoid stitching around the zipper pull.

- Most zippers have a stitching line woven into the tape. Although not always easy to sew, making use of this line keeps stitching centered.

- To avoid puckering at the bottom of the zipper, stitch each side beginning at the lower edge of the zipper and working toward the top.

- Finish all seams before inserting the zipper (except when using invisible zippers).

- Be sure seam allowances are at least ⅝" (15.9mm) where the zipper is inserted. Add fabric if necessary.

- Avoid sewing close to zipper coils/teeth so the fabric does not get caught when using the zipper.

LAPPED ZIPPER

A lapped zipper has one side, the lap, that is not sewn down and is used to cover the zipper. The top can be left open when used in skirts, pants or the center back of dresses. The top is closed when used under arms and in a side seam in a dress.

The lapped zipper is sewn in conjunction with the seam allowance where it is placed. Beginning at the bottom of the garment, sew the garment seam using a ⅝" (15.9mm) seam allowance and a regular stitch length. When you come to the point where the bottom of the zipper will be, stop and backstitch.

For example, if inserting a lapped zipper in the center back of a dress, sew the back dress seam, stopping and backstitching where the bottom of the zipper will be. From this point, baste the rest of the seam, maintaining the ⅝" (15.9mm) seam allowance all the way to the top of the dress. Press the seam open.

Change to a zipper foot. Extend the right seam allowance away from the remaining seam and garment fabric. Place the closed zipper right-side-down with the zipper coils next to the seam. Pin in place.

Adjust the needle to a far right position so the needle falls approximately ¼" (6.4mm) from the edge of the zipper tape. Beginning at the bottom of the zipper, sew the right zipper tape to the extended seam allowance.

Fold the zipper back along the previously stitched line, creating a small fold. Adjust your needle position and stitch close to the folded edge along the entire zipper.

To finish and create the *lap*, unfold the fabric and lay the zipper flat. Adjust the needle position to sew ⅜" (9.5mm) from the seam line. Lower the needle into the seamline at the bottom of the zipper. Backstitch and sew ⅜" (9.5mm) out from the seam line; pivot and continue stitching to the top of the seam. Pull thread tails to the wrong side and tie off. Rip out the basting stitches on the garment to access the zipper.

With the seam allowance extended, place the closed zipper right-side-down with the zipper coils next to the seam.

On the right side of the zipper, continue sewing the lap to the top of the zipper, maintaining ⅜" (9.5mm) from the basted seam.

 sewing 101

If your machine does not have adjustable needle position, use an adjustable zipper foot. The adjustable zipper foot can be set to sew on the right or left side of the zipper by adjusting the foot and tightening the thumbscrew. Adjustments can be made that allow the foot to sew close to the zipper.

CENTERED ZIPPER

Centered zippers are the most commonly used styles. Taking care to make both sides of the zipper identical will result in professional looking results.

With the regular presser foot, sew the seam below the zipper area and backtack at both ends. Change to a basting stitch and continue sewing the seam. Press the seam open and place the right side of the zipper against the seam allowance. Zipper coils should be centered over the seam. Pin to seam allowances only.

Attach the zipper foot and move the needle position far left or right as needed, or adjust the foot. Sew through tape and seam allowances only (not the garment) on each side. Lay the garment right-side-up. Pin through all the layers of seam allowance, zipper tape and garment. Adjust the needle position or foot, and topstitch along the left side of the zipper from bottom to top. Begin at the seam line, stitch out ¼" (6.4mm), pivot, and continue topstitching. Repeat for the opposite side. If your zipper foot has a guide, adjust the guide for accurate topstitching.

Topstitch along the bottom seam line, pivot and continue down the second side.

sewing 101

If your zipper foot has a guide, try making tucks using the zipper foot. Use the guide to sew evenly spaced tuck lines.

Mark each tuck, and fold the fabric on the marked line. Move the needle position to the far left and adjust the guide the desired distance to the right. Place fabric under the foot with the fold to the right, and stitch.

INVISIBLE ZIPPER

Invisible zippers provide the most unobtrusive closing—the only part that shows when they are closed is the narrow pull tab. The right and the wrong side of the zipper is not easily recognized, so mark the right side with fabric chalk before sewing.

To insert properly, the coils need to lie as flat as possible before stitching. Take the time to first prepare the zipper to achieve the best results. Open the zipper all the way. From the wrong side, iron the zipper flat so the two rows of stitching show. Use a low iron setting, being careful not to touch the coils with the iron.

There are different methods for inserting an invisible zipper. After trying several methods, choose the one most comfortable for you. One easy method is to insert the invisible zipper before closing the seam line. Attach an invisible zipper foot to the machine, select a straight stitch, a 2.5mm stitch length and place the needle in the center position.

Mark the point where the seam will end and the zipper will begin. Open the zipper completely, and pin the right side of the zipper to the right side of the seam allowance. The wrong side of the zipper tape will be on top while you are sewing. Place the coil on the ⅝" (15.9mm) seam line and the top stop of the zipper ¾" (19mm) below the cut edge of the fabric. Lower the presser foot and guide the right groove of the foot over the coil. Beginning at the top and sewing toward the bottom, stitch the zipper to the fabric. Stop at the marked spot (when the foot hits the slider).

Repeat for the other side, matching the right side of the zipper tape to the right side of the fabric, with the coil on the ⅝" (15.9mm) seam line and the top stop of the zipper ¾" (19mm) below the cut edge of the fabric. Place the left groove of the foot over the coil and stitch, stopping at the marked spot.

To finish stitching the seamline, close the zipper and attach a general presser foot. Stitch the seam allowance to the zipper, stitching as close as possible to the zipper. The closed zipper now forms one continual line with the seam of your garment.

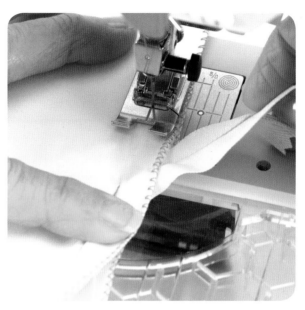

With a general presser foot, stitch the seam allowance to the zipper, stitching as close as possible to the zipper.

From the wrong side, iron the zipper flat, being careful to keep the iron away from the coils.

 sewing 101

Instead of using pins to hold the zipper while sewing, use matte-finish invisible tape or basting tape.

Repeat for the other side, matching the right side of the zipper tape to the right side of the fabric.

6

embellishments

Many decorative stitches that were once sewn by hand can be duplicated using the sewing machine. Whether you favor heirloom sewing or simply wish to add a few personalized details, using your machine to the fullest is a true timesaver. The sewing machine settings will vary depending on your machine, your fabric and the result you hope to achieve. Unleash your creativity and use it to the fullest!

FAGOTING

Fagoting is a small space between two fabric pieces filled with decorative stitches, creating an open, lace-type effect. Use fagoting to join laces, fabrics, or even lace to fabric. A variety of stitch patterns can be used for fagoting, but it's best to choose a pattern that makes several side-to-side stitches, such as a honeycomb, feather, slanted pin or fagoting stitch. A zigzag stitch may produce problems as it pulls the two fabrics together, having only stitches going side to side.

Fagoting width varies from ⅛"–⅜" (3.2mm–9.5mm) and can increase the size of the fabric. Take this into consideration and make any necessary adjustments to the pattern and fabric before cutting. Remember, your finished piece will be larger after adding fagoting.

Select thread and needle according to fabric weight (see chart on page 145). Use rayon thread for luster or cotton thread for strength. Also think outside the box and experiment with specialty threads—each can give varying results. For lightweight fabrics, use needle size 70/9 or 80/11 and a finer thread. Topstitching thread and buttonhole twist used with needle size 90/14 work best on heavyweight fabrics.

Choose a foot with a wide opening to accommodate the wider stitches. A clear embroidery foot, zigzag foot or open-toe presser foot will hold both fabrics securely, have an adequately-sized opening and provide good visibility. Cording can also be added to the fagoted edges by using a pin-tuck foot.

Loosen upper tension to number 1 or 2 so the top threads will pull slightly to the bottom of the fabric. Stitch length determines the density of fagoting space. A shorter length gives a fuller, more filled-in space. The stitch width determines the size of the opening. A larger width gives a wider space. Sew a test on scrap fabric first, and make notes of stitch length, tension setting, or needle size for future reference. Begin with a stitch width of 5mm and a satin stitch length. Adjust as necessary.

(continued on next page...)

FAGOTING SETTINGS

Foot: Zigzag, open-toe or embroidery

Needle: Appropriate for fabric and thread

Stitch: Decorative stitch of choice

Stitch length: Varies with stitch

Stitch width: Varies with stitch

 sewing 101

Heirloom sewing is usually sewn on sheer, lightweight fabrics such as batiste or light cottons trimmed with tucks, smocking, narrow ribbons or an assortment of lace. It can imitate fine, hand-worked fagoting. Choose a stitch pattern to complement your project.

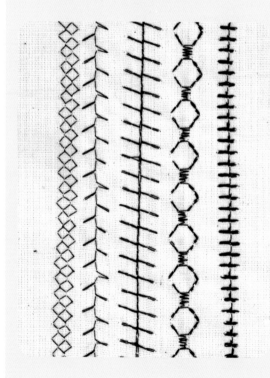

(Fagoting continued...)

Fold the raw edge of each fabric under ½" (12.7mm). Spray starch and press to stiffen. With the folded edges of the two fabrics about ⅛"–⅜ " (3.2mm–9.5mm) apart (depending on the selected stitch width), begin stitching. A fagoting stitch will catch one fabric edge, stitch across the space between fabrics, and stitch into the other folded edge. Adjust the stitch width and keep the fabric evenly spaced so the stitches just catch the fabric edges. Press.

Select a straight stitch or a small decorative stitch and anchor the fagoting stitching to the fabric by sewing down each side. Trim any excess fabric close to the stitching.

Perfect fagoting depends on maintaining an even space between fabrics. Use the guide lines on the machine or a fagoting plate, if available. Anything that sufficiently keeps fabric edges apart may be usable. Even a coffee stirring stick taped in front of the foot helps maintain appropriate spacing.

Finished fagoting with lace

A coffee stirring stick taped in front of the foot helps maintain appropriate spacing.

Fagoting with lace requires more accuracy and preparation; lace is normally open weave and soft, and can easily pull and distort. Prepare the lace with spray starch and press until stiff, keeping the lace straight. If working on curves, gently press into the curved shape. If more stability is necessary, lightly fuse both edges with water-soluble stabilizer, always maintaining the proper spacing.

When fagoting laces with corded edgings, use a five or seven groove pin-tuck foot. Place the cording headed either right or left of center. Try using a twin needle for an entirely different fagoting effect.

CORDED FAGOTING

Corded fagoting gives a finished look to each edge with a raised edge. Cording can be sewn on each edge while sewing the fagoting. Another alternative is to sew the cording to the folded edges of each piece before fagoting. To sew cording to the folded edge, select a narrow zigzag stitch width of 2.5mm, and a satin stitch length of 1mm or less. Place cord against the edge and begin sewing. Repeat for the other edge. The finished corded edges are now ready for fagoting.

sewing 101

Buttonhole and carpet thread is a perfect size for dainty corded fagoting.

CORDED FAGOTING SETTINGS

Foot: Zigzag, open-toe or embroidery

Needle: Appropriate for fabric and thread

Stitch: Zigzag

Stitch length: 0mm–1mm

Stitch width: 2.5mm

Place cord against the edge and begin sewing.

FAGOTING WITH A TAILOR TACK FOOT

A tailor tack (fringe) foot provides a quick method of fagoting. Select a zigzag stitch with a width of 5mm or more, and a satin stitch length of 1mm or less. Decrease the upper tension to 1 or 2. Place the fabric right sides together and sew with a 5⁄8" (15.9mm) seam. Sew slowly and smoothly.

FAGOTING SETTINGS (WITH A TAILOR TACK FOOT)

Foot: Tailor tack (fringe)

Needle: Appropriate for fabric and thread

Stitch: Zigzag

Stitch length: 0mm–1mm

Stitch width: 3mm–5mm

Open the two layers and press seam allowances open. Anchor the fagoting to each side with a straight stitch or small decorative stitch, sewing along the fagoted edge.

Lastly, bundle the fagoting stitches with a straight stitch, such as the triple straight-stitch or straight stretch stitch. Attach an embroidery open-toe foot, and center the foot over the fagoting stitches. Sew down the middle. The stitches will begin bundling together.

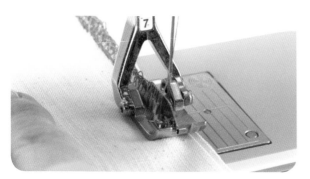

Place the fabric right sides together and sew down the edge with a 5⁄8" (15.9mm) seam.

TWIN NEEDLE PIN TUCKS

Twin needles used in conjunction with the pin-tuck foot create raised, evenly spaced rows of tucks. Use one thread color in both needles, or try two different colors for contrast. Add cording for a more emphasized raised effect.

Grooves on the bottom of the pin-tuck foot run the length of the sole, providing even, parallel spacing between pin-tuck rows. Pin-tuck feet are available with 3, 5, 7 and 9 grooves. Select the number of grooves based on the fabric weight, and then choose an appropriately sized twin needle. The needle size will be larger than the groove size. For example, the 3-groove foot has 3mm wide grooves, but will use the 4mm twin needle.

Use a straight stitch with a 1.5mm–2mm length. Walk the handwheel slowly to ensure the stitch will not hit the foot once the needle is inserted.

- **3-groove:** 3mm-wide grooves, use 4.0/80mm twin needle. Use primarily on medium- to heavyweight fabrics (wool, denim, corduroy). Can be used for small piping and passementerie. A triple needle can be used with the 3-groove pin-tuck foot.

- **5-groove:** 2mm-wide grooves, use 2.5/80 or 3.0/90 twin needle. Use primarily on medium-weight fabrics. This foot can also be used for inserting invisible zippers. More versatile for general sewing.

TWIN NEEDLE PIN TUCK SETTINGS

Foot: Pin-tuck

Needle: Twin appropriate for foot

Stitch: Straight

Stitch length: 1.7mm–2mm

Stitch width: 0mm

Note: *Engage double needle function, if available.*

- **7-groove:** 1.3mm-wide grooves, use 2.0/80 twin needle. Use primarily on fine and lightweight fabrics, and for stitching miniature fagoting and entredeux.

- **9-groove:** 1mm-wide grooves, use 1.6/70 twin needle. Use primarily for sheer and lightweight fabrics. Use for small corded pin tucks and smocking.

sewing 101

The first number of a twin needle is the distance in millimeters between the two needles, and the second number refers to the size of the needle itself. The smaller the number, the smaller and finer the needle.

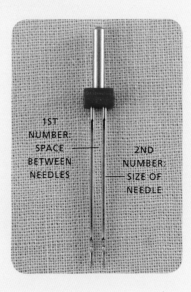

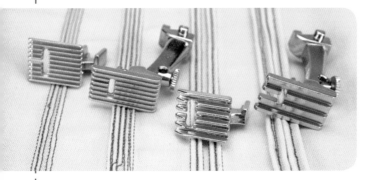

9-groove, 7-groove, 5-groove and 3-groove pin-tuck feet

Sewing Straight Pin Tucks

Pin tucks are created as the bobbin thread pulls the line of stitching in closer, creating ridges that fit into the grooves. Pin tucks require using two spools of thread with a twin needle. Consult the owner's manual for specific threading guidelines for your machine. Your machine may eliminate the second threading through one of the thread guides.

Attach the foot and insert the proper size twin needle. Select the twin needle function if available on your machine. If not available, hand crank the needle manually through the first stitch to avoid breaking the needles, and adjust the width if necessary.

Thread your machine with two spools of thread on separate spool pins. To prevent tangling, feed the left spool from the back and the right spool from the front. Sew a few sample stitches on scrap fabric to check stitch length and tension. Tightening the tension can increase the pin-tuck effect.

Mark the first line of stitching with a removable marking pen, following the fabric grainline. Or pull a thread to follow for the first tuck (see page 64). Align the center of the pin-tuck foot over the placement line. Sew the first row accurately as each subsequent tuck depends on the straightness of the first. The first row will be sewn in the center of the foot.

Continue to sew the number of pin tucks needed. For each new row, place the previously sewn tuck into a groove right or left of center. Pin tucks can be spaced further apart by using every other groove, or placing the right side of the foot against the last tuck made.

sewing 101

Most machines have a vertical and a horizontal thread spool, but if your machine does not have two, place a freestanding thread stand behind the machine for the second spool.

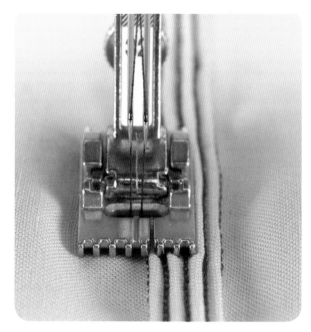

For each new row, place the previously sewn tuck into the next groove.

Place pin tucks further apart by placing the right side of the foot against the last tuck made.

Sewing Pin-Tucked Curves and Corners

Take the time to sew curves and corners accurately. Move slowly around curves, sewing carefully. From time to time, stop with the tips of the needles in the fabric, lift the presser foot and adjust the fabric around the curve.

For corners, stitch until the inner needle reaches the corner, and lower the feed dogs. With the tips of the needles in the fabric, raise the presser foot and pivot the fabric 45 degrees. Lower the foot and take one stitch. Raise the foot and again pivot 45 degrees to completely turn the corner. Raise the feed dogs and continue sewing.

Scalloped pin tucks are easily made using the machine's built-in scallop stitch pattern. Add them at the bottom of hems, on edges or anywhere a bit of texture is desired. Always check the stitch width to ensure the needle doesn't hit the foot.

Crosshatched pin tucks are created by alternating the direction of rows while sewing over previously made pin tucks. Sew the desired number of rows in one direction across your fabric. Turn the fabric 90 degrees. Sew the second set of rows perpendicular to and crossing over the first set.

sewing 101

Whenever selecting a decorative stitch pattern, check the stitch width to ensure the needle does not hit the side of the pin-tuck foot. You don't want to break your needles just as you get started.

Pivot the fabric 45 degrees. Lower the foot and take one stitch.

Raise the foot and again pivot 45 degrees to completely turn the corner.

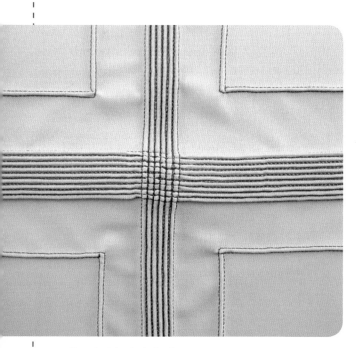

Crosshatched pin tucks

CORDED PIN TUCKS

Fill pin tucks with cording, such as gimp or pearl cotton, to increase the raised effect. The cording size should match the groove size on the foot. For a more prominent raised effect, tighten the upper tension.

Most machines will draw the cording from underneath, allowing the cording to move accurately and easily under the groove in the foot. To thread the cording in this way, lower the feed dogs and remove the needle plate. Thread the cording from under the plate, through the bobbin area and up through the hole right in front of the needle opening. Replace the needle plate and raise the feed dogs without unthreading the cord. Keep the bobbin door cover open to allow the cord to move freely.

If your needle plate doesn't have a hole in front of the needle opening, bypass this step and insert the cording directly under the fabric and within the foot groove. Pull the cord under the foot and toward the back, under the center groove. Sew the first tuck. The cord feeds under the pin-tuck foot and is encased by the bobbin thread. Repeat for additional rows, always tucking the previous tuck into a groove and the new cording in the center groove.

You can also use this technique to make smocking (see page 127).

sewing 101

A quilting bar will aid in keeping rows straight and evenly spaced. After sewing the first row, insert the guide bar onto the appropriate foot (varies by machine). Adjust the bar to the left or right so it's aligned with the first row of stitching. Sew, keeping the bar aligned with the reference line.

CORDED PIN TUCK SETTINGS

Foot: Pin-tuck

Needle: Twin appropriate for foot

Stitch: Straight

Stitch length: 1.5mm–3.5mm

Stitch width: 0mm

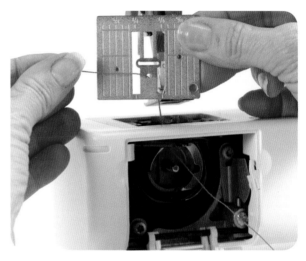

Some needle plates have a specialty hole in front of the needle hole. Thread cording through this hole.

Place cording under the fabric and in the center groove. Stitch pin tucks over the cording.

HEMSTITCHING

Hemstitching was a work of art during the early 1900s. The technique involved pulling threads from the fabric and *bundling* the remaining parallel threads using needle and thread to create an open design. You can achieve a similar effect with your machine, a wing needle and a decorative stitch pattern. Experiment with various patterns such as the cross-stitch, daisy or the hemstitch if available on your machine.

Use a single wing needle, size 100 for most fabrics, although larger size 120 works best for loosely woven fabrics such as linens. If a wing needle is unavailable, use a large universal or topstitching size 120/19 needle and select a stitch that returns to the same hole several times. This emphasizes and reinforces the decorative holes made by the needle. A partially overlapping zigzag stitch can also produce hemstitching. Spray the fabric with spray starch and press to slightly stiffen. Insert a single wing needle and select a zigzag stitch with a width of 1.75mm–2mm, and a length of 1mm–1.25mm. Use a zigzag foot or any open foot for the best visibility. Sew each row slowly and hold the fabric taut in front of and behind the needle.

Stitch down the first row to the desired length. Stop with the needle tip down on the left side of a zigzag stitch. Raise the presser foot and turn the fabric 180 degrees. Lower the presser foot and stitch next to the previous row, guiding the fabric so the left side of the stitch enters the holes on the right side of the previous stitching (the center holes).

Besides the zigzag, other stitches can create a hemstitch, such as a picot, daisy, ladder and cross-stitch. Two of the most popular stitch patterns are Venetian and Parisian. When using a Venetian or a built-in hemstitch pattern, the need for sewing multiple rows is eliminated; the stitches automatically go in and out the same holes with both sides sewn at the same time.

HEMSTITCH SETTINGS

Foot: Zigzag, open-toe, edgestitch or cording

Needle: Single wing (hemstitch)

Stitch: Decorative stitch

Stitch length: 1mm–1.25mm

Stitch width: 1.75mm–2mm

Using a single wing needle, stitch down the first row to the desired length.

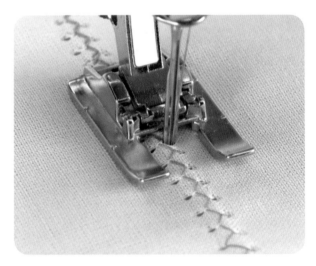

Turn and stitch next to the first row so the needle goes into the same center hole.

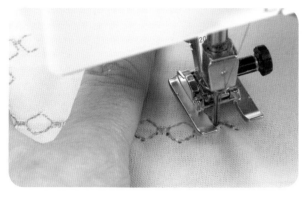

Hemstitch around a corner by walking the needle.

Hemstitching Corners

When turning corners, walk the needle around the corner for several stitches. To walk, lift the presser foot just enough to move the fabric and lower it, and manually turn the hand wheel for each stitch. As with any added embellishment, a foot with a wide viewing area is always helpful.

Hemstitching a Single Fold Hem

Add a lovely finish to a hem. The hem can be a single fold or a double fold (see instructions at right), with the single fold giving a softer hem. Use a single or a double wing needle.

Finish the raw edge with a serger, zigzag or overlock stitch. Fold and press a single fold hem. Select a stitch pattern. Stitch ¼" (6.4mm) from the hem edge, sewing on the right side of fabric. At the end of the hem, turn and stitch a second pass directly on top of the first stitches so that the needle falls into the same holes; this widens the hemstitch. Trim the fabric close to the stitches on the wrong side. Try using a double hemstitch needle for a different effect.

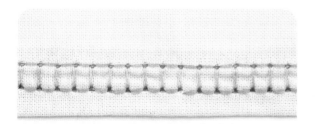

Finished single fold hemstitched hem

Hemstitching a Double Fold Hem

A double fold hem is also sewn on the right side of fabric. Fold the hem twice and press. Stitch so that one side of the stitch enters the hem allowance and the other side enters the single layer of fabric. At the end of the hem, turn and stitch a second pass directly on top of the first stitches so that the needle falls into the same holes; this widens the hemstitch.

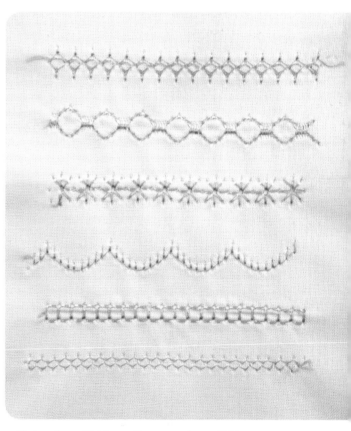

Various hemstitching patterns may be available on your machine.

CORDED HEMSTITCHING

Hemstitching over cord makes the stitching stand out, especially if the cording is a contrasting color. Experiment with pearl cotton no. 5 and no. 8, or try several strands of embroidery thread. Use a multi-cording foot which guides the cords to the left and right of center and keeps it securely in place.

Slide the cords into the appropriate slots of the foot, depending on the stitch width. Stitch the first row, guiding the cord so the stitch to the side couches over it. At the end of the row, pivot the needle and stitch a second row to partially overlap the first. The second sewing pass also enlarges the holes for a more distinct effect.

The beginning and ending corded hemstitching is most often hidden within a seam, but for situations where this isn't the case, leave a long tail. Thread the tail into a hand-sewing needle with a large eye, and pull the tail to the back of the fabric. Weave about ½" (12.7mm) of it into the stitches to secure. Trim excess cord.

CORDED HEMSTITCH SETTINGS

Foot: Multi-cording or cording

Needle: Single wing (hemstitch)

Stitch: Decorative

Stitch length: 1mm–1.25mm

Stitch width: 1.75mm–2mm

 sewing 101

Polyester fabrics are very difficult to hemstitch. If they are a "must," do so in very small areas, choose a simple stitch pattern to avoid puckering, loosen upper tension, use a large-sized universal needle instead of a wing needle, and use spray starch to fully stiffen.

MACHINE-CROCHETED EDGING

While growing up, doilies with lovely crocheted edging covered tables and chairs. Many were the handiwork of my grandmother and mother. This lovely edging also creates beautiful handkerchiefs.

MACHINE-CROCHETED EDGE SETTINGS

Foot: Open-toe or embroidery

Needle: Universal 90/14, or appropriate for thread

Stitch: Blanket

Stitch length: varies

Stitch width: 3mm–5mm (or more if your machine goes up to 9mm)

Although not truly crochet, you can replicate the look of crocheted lace on edges with your sewing machine. After finishing the first row, add a second or third row for a more predominant effect. Alter the appearance by changing to a different decorative stitch for subsequent rows.

Vintage handkerchiefs with crocheted edging

Making Machine-Crocheted Tape

Make machine-crocheted tape and sew it to ready-made garments or use it as a hem. To make machine-crocheted tape, use heavyweight water-soluble stabilizer, 12 weight thread, twill tape, and a universal sewing machine needle size 90/14. Set the stitch width between 3mm and 9mm as desired. A wider stitch width creates a longer crocheted edge.

Cut stabilizer strips the length of the twill tape and at least 2" (5cm) wide. Place ¼" (6.4mm) of stabilizer under the twill tape and the remainder extending off the side of the tape. Using a blanket stitch, sew along the edge of the twill tape (through the stabilizer), with the left stitch just catching the edge of the tape.

When the first row of stitching is completed, select a straight stitch and sew along the edges of the stitching on the twill tape.

To add additional rows, select the blanket stitch and sew a row to the right of the previous blanket stitches, catching the edges with the new stitches to join. Continue adding rows as desired. Rinse away stabilizer when finished.

Use the finished tape to embellish the edge of napkins, handkerchiefs, or even necklines. To use, sew the tape directly onto the fabric edge.

Embellishing the Edge

Instead of sewing stitches along the edge of twill tape, stitch the machine-crocheted edging directly along the edge of your sewing project or a plain handkerchief. Using the same method as above, sew machine-crocheted edging directly onto the edge of your sewing project instead of twill tape.

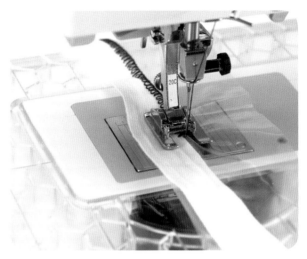

Using a blanket stitch, sew along the edge of the twill tape.

Continue adding rows as desired, the left stitch just catching the edge of the previous row of stitches.

sewing 101

If you don't have heavyweight water-soluble stabilizer, use at least four layers of regular weight stabilizer. Place the layers between sheets of waxed paper and gently touch with a warm iron to fuse into one sheet.

ENTREDEUX

Entredeux means *between two* in French. Entredeux is a narrow trim with tiny square holes down the center of a batiste strip. It's used as trim between two seam edges, or for joining lace to fabric, lace to lace or fabric to fabric. Entredeux can be purchased ready-made, or you can create your own with a 110/18 wing needle and your sewing machine's built-in stitch patterns. Try a variety of stitches to create the effect you desire. Some stitches to start with are Venetian, entredeux, cross-stitch or even the daisy pattern.

You will use cotton organdy, batiste or similar lightweight fabric, 60 weight cotton thread, cording and a single wing needle. Try no. 5 pearl cotton thread, buttonhole twist, several strands of embroidery floss or button thread. Use a 5-groove cording foot to keep the cording exactly where it needs to be.

When sewing entredeux, engage the twin needle function on your machine, if available, to prevent the wings from hitting the foot. Select Venetian or another decorative stitch pattern. Adjust the stitch width and length according to the chosen stitch. For example, begin with a 2.5mm stitch width and 3mm stitch length for the entredeux stitch.

Making Entredeux

Cut a 2" (5cm) wide strip of fabric, the length determined by the finished project. Fold the strip in half with raw edges together and press lightly. This crease provides a center line to follow. Do not add cording yet. Select the preferred decorative stitch, sew one row down the center and stop. Raise the presser foot with the needle down. Pivot 180 degrees. Align the needle to ensure that it will fall within the previous holes, and get ready to sew the second row. (This widens the holes and provides the second edged side.)

ENTREDEUX SETTINGS

Foot: Cording, open-toe or zigzag

Needle: Single wing (hemstitch)

Stitch: Zigzag, triple zigzag, Venetian, entredeux, other decorative

Stitch length: Varies with stitch pattern

Stitch width: Varies with stitch pattern

Note: *It's possible to use an edgestitch or open-toe foot for this technique, but it's much easier with a cording foot.*

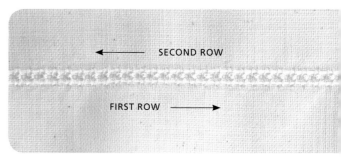

Machine-made entredeux

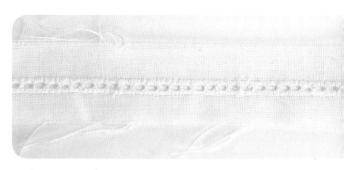

Vintage entredeux

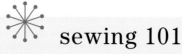

sewing 101

Stitching on the bias allows holes to open easier. Stabilizer can be used for temporary hold and support while stitching.

Place the cording in grooves 2 and 4 of the foot. (If using a foot other than a cording foot, sew very slowly while keeping the cording in place with your hands.) The cording thread fills the outer edges of stitching, creating a look similar to purchased entredeux. The entredeux can now be attached to lace or to fabric.

If your machine has the Venetian stitch pattern, one sewing pass is all that's necessary to create the entredeux. Place the cording into the farthest outside slots of the cording foot and select the Venetian stitch. Sew once down the center of your 2" (5cm) strip to complete the entredeux.

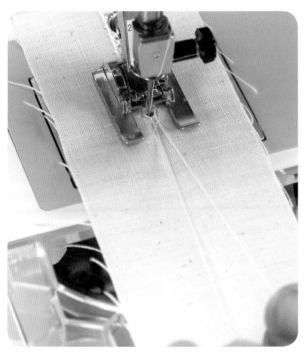

If not using a cording foot, sew very slowly while keeping the cording in place with your hands.

Attaching Entredeux to Lace

Before sewing entredeux to lace or fabric, test sew a sample to determine the proper stitch length and width. Stitches must fall within the holes of the entredeux. To test, cut a 5" (13cm) strip of entredeux. Select a decorative stitch and set a 3mm stitch width and a 2.5mm stitch length. Begin sewing, stopping every few stitches to adjust the stitch length as necessary until the needle enters each hole of entredeux. Jot down the machine setting for future reference. Each decorative stitch you work with will have different settings.

After testing for stitch length and width, select a foot that will hold the entredeux and lace securely, such as the zigzag, appliqué or pin-tuck foot. Trim the seam from one side of the entredeux strip, trimming up to the stitches. Butt that seam against the lace edge. Sew a narrow, short zigzag stitch, with the zigzag going from the entredeux hole to the lace. If puckering occurs, place tear-away stabilizer underneath both the lace and entredeux.

Sew a narrow, fine zigzag stitch, going from the entredeux hole to the lace.

Attaching Entredeux to Fabric

When sewing entredeux to fabric, don't trim the seam edge from the entredeux. Place the raw edge of entredeux right sides together with the fabric edge. Select a straight stitch and sew in the seam ditch close to the entredeux. Trim both fabric edges to about ⅛" (3.2mm) wide.

Select a small zigzag stitch with a width of 2.5mm–3mm and a length of 1mm. While sewing, one swing should fall over the edge of the fabric, and the other swing should fall next to the entredeux. You may need to adjust the stitch width and length accordingly.

Open flat and press the *roll* toward the fabric. An optional stitch can be added to prevent the seam from rolling. Select a zigzag with a stitch width and length of 1mm. With fabric right-side-up, begin sewing. One swing of the zigzag should go into entredeux and the other swing into the fabric.

Attaching Entredeux to Puffing

Cut the entredeux strip to the desired length and iron with spray starch. Trim one seam allowance to ¼" (6.4mm). Place the puffing and entredeux strip right sides together, aligning the raw edges. Select a straight stitch and sew next to the entredeux holes. Trim the seam allowance to ⅛" (3.2mm). For more information on puffing, see page 116.

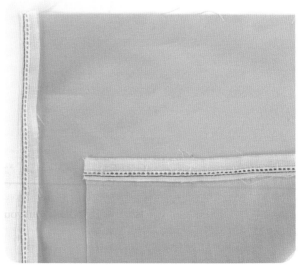

Entredeux attached to fabric, ready for next steps

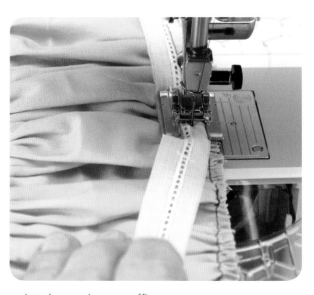

Attach entredeux to puffing

more from the past

I love to browse through older pattern books to get new and unique sewing ideas! Any book you choose will be filled with new techniques to try. Throughout the years, carefully placed embellishments lent a decorative flair to gowns, baby clothes, costumes and everyday wear. Puffing and ruches were favorites during the eighteenth and nineteenth centuries. Intricately embroidered lace, called handlooms, added a delicate effect wherever they were added.

CUTWORK

This lovely handwork has been around for centuries, and will be treasured for years to come. Cutwork is an embellishment technique that can be replicated using your sewing machine, rather than done by hand. Cutwork has open, cutout design areas outlined with satin stitching. Bars are connecting stitches used in open areas to add stability and interest to the design. These detailed designs can be used as accents on blouses, cuffs, yokes and hem areas. Try adding cutwork to a table runner for a beautiful table setting. When receiving all the admiration of your gorgeous handiwork, don't let on how quickly it was made.

Cutwork begins with a design that can be as simple or elaborate as you wish. Designs are available, but you can create your own. If making a new sewing project, stitch out the cutwork design before cutting any pattern pieces. This allows you to properly place the cutwork design where you want it on the finished project.

CUTWORK SETTINGS

Foot: Free-motion, embroidery or open-toe

Needle: Appropriate for fabric

Stitch: Satin stitch or straight stitch

Stitch length: 0mm

Stitch width: 2mm–5mm

Straight stitch around the drawn outline several times.

Original cutwork design and completed cutwork butterfly motif

For this technique, it's best to work with fabrics that don't ravel easily. Cutwork traditionally is done on fine linen, cotton or lawn fabric. Use all-purpose thread for straight-stitch outlining, cotton or rayon thread for satin stitching, and needle size 70/10 or 80/12. Attach a free-motion, embroidery or open-toe foot, and use a hoop to prevent puckering.

Whether using a commercial design or one you created, transfer a mirror image of the design onto heavyweight water-soluble stabilizer with a fabric marking pen. Baste the stabilizer to the wrong side of the fabric. Place the fabric in the hoop with the stabilizer facing up.

Place the hoop under the foot—you may have to remove the foot to insert the hoop. Select a straight stitch and a short stitch length, and outline the design several times to stabilize.

(continued on next page...)

113

(Cutwork continued...)

Remove the fabric and stabilizer from the hoop. Using sharp appliqué or embroidery scissors, cut away the fabric from open areas of the design, staying ¹/₁₆" (1.2mm) away from the stitches.

Re-hoop the fabric and stabilizer, and place the piece back under the foot. Within each open area, stitch design bars using a straight stitch (see page 136 on making Richelieu bars). Stitch three or four rows for stability in each opening, following your selected design. Select a narrow zigzag stitch, just wide enough to cover the straight bars. Satin stitch over each bar.

Continue to satin stitch around the design's outline, covering all the previous straight stitching. Working from the center out reduces the tendency to pucker. Remove from the hoop and trim excess stabilizer from the back. Rinse in warm water to remove all the stabilizer. Your cutwork design is complete and ready to be placed onto your pattern pieces.

A readymade garment will stand out with your handiwork by inserting cutwork. Add to the neckline or near the hem. To do this, follow the instructions previously given, and when ready to place in the hoop, insert the garment instead of fabric.

Cut away the fabric from open areas of the design.

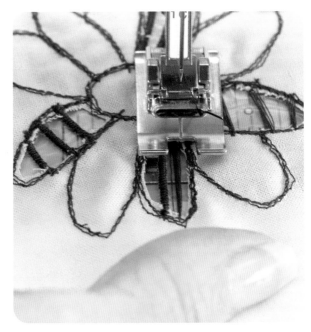

Satin stitch over each bar ensuring you encase all the threads.

HANDLOOMS

Handlooms are beautifully embroidered strips that can be inserted between fabrics to embellish sleeves, yokes or skirts. *Handloom* also refers to highly embellished scarfs or coverlets. These embroidered strips are traditionally made with a handloom, which keeps yarns taut while the design is woven directly into the fabric.

You can replicate the look of handloom trim or fabric using all the built-in stitches your sewing machine has to offer. It's a wonderful way to test sew all those lovely built-in stitches.

Stitching is done on a base fabric, such as silk, batiste, batik, cotton or even ribbon. A variety of threads are available to try, such as embroidery, metallic, pearl cotton or variegated thread. You choose the base fabric, the thread and the design. Even the width of the finished handloom is up to you!

Select a base fabric. Determine the length and width based on how you will use the finished handloom. Most often, it will be inserted between other fabrics, so allow at least a ½" (12.7mm) seam allowance on each side of the embroidered design. Draw a design with fabric marking pencil directly onto the base fabric.

Select the decorative stitch you wish to use and stitch a test sample. Is the design too large, too small? Can the stitch width and length be adjusted for a better look? Are the stitches puckering? If so, place water-soluble stabilizer underneath and check the tension.

When you have the stitch perfected, begin sewing by following the drawn lines. Whether you sew one row, or alternate rows of designs and thread colors, the finished handloom will enhance your next sewing project.

HANDLOOM SETTINGS

Foot: Embroidery, open-toe or zigzag

Needle: Appropriate for fabric and thread

Stitch: Decorative

Stitch length: Varies with stitch pattern

Stitch width: Varies with stitch pattern

Draw a design with fabric marking pencil directly onto the base fabric.

Completed handlooms

PUFFING

During the nineteenth century, dresses were adorned with ruches, lace, bustles and puffing. Most often, the stitched puffing edges were hidden with laces, both straight and gathered. Puffing can be seen in the bottom section of very full and elaborate dresses, or along the bottom of sleeves next to long and deep ruffling.

Determine the finished width and length of the puffing strip. Choose a fabric type to complement the finished project. Due to the fullness of the puffing and added edging, lightweight fabrics are usually the best choice. To determine the length of the puffing strip, generally start with twice the length of the finished size. The width of the puffing is your choice based on the pattern design.

Cut fabric strips to the desired width and length. Select a straight stitch with a length of 3mm–5mm. Loosen upper tension. Stitch two rows ⅛" (3.2mm) apart along both long edges of the strip, staying ¼" (6.4mm) from the raw edge. Leave long thread tails at the end of both stitching rows.

PUFFING SETTINGS

Foot: Open-toe or wide gathering

Needle: Universal appropriate for fabric

Stitch: Straight

Stitch length: 3mm–5mm (basting)

Stitch width: 0mm

Pull on these thread tails on each side until the desired fullness is achieved. Even out the gathers and tie knots in the thread at each end to secure.

To insert the puffing strip between two other fabrics, place the puffing right sides together with a second fabric, and sew together using a standard stitch length and a ⅝" (15.9mm) seam allowance. Trim the seam allowance to ¼" (6.4mm). Turn to the right side and finger press open. To hide the seam line, sew lace or embroidered trim over the seam. An added effect is achieved by adding gathered lace to one edge of the puffing.

Finished puffing piece

Pull on the thread tails to gather the strip.

Sew lace or trim over the seam.

RUCHING

Ruches are ribbons or fabric strips that are gathered through the center and sewn down to create elaborate embellishments on dresses. Traditionally, the edges were hemmed, had a decorative stitch or were elaborately covered with laces and ribbons. Typically, ruches were 1"–2" (2.5cm–5cm) wide, but they can be made in any width and are suitable for any purpose.

Ruching strips can be cut either on the bias or straight of grain. Experiment with both, as each produces a different result. Before gathering, hem or serge both lengthwise edges, or add trim to cover.

Select a basting stitch. Sew a row of stitches down the center of the strip, bartacking at the beginning. If the strip is long, break the sewing into sections for easier gathering. Leave a thread tail at least 6" (15cm) at the end. Pull the thread at one end to gather the strip. Tie off.

Select a standard stitch length. Place the gathered strip onto your fabric and sew down the center to secure. Add some ruches to your favorite garment or even a purse!

RUCHING SETTINGS

Foot: Open-toe or zigzag

Needle: Appropriate for fabric

Stitch: Straight

Stitch length: 3mm–5mm (basting)

Stitch width: 0mm

Bartack at the beginning, and then sew down the center of the strip with a basting stitch.

Several different kinds of ruches

surface and thread embellishments

Embellishments are decorative details that add a personal flair to your sewing. Instead of spending hours hand sewing elaborate embroidery and raised embellishments, we can take advantage of our sewing machine, specialty feet and eye-catching trims, allowing us to work fast while still being creative!

WORKING WITH SPECIAL THREADS AND TRIMS

There are many types of specialty notions available today, and all can facilitate unlimited creativity. Just knowing some helpful tips will result in works of art, rather than a lot of unfinished projects lying in drawers. Before trying new techniques and notions on an actual sewing project, pull out scrap fabric and play around. Get comfortable with the materials.

Threads are available in metallics, silks, ribbons and fluorescents, many full of luster and shimmer. Adding metallic ribbon or using embroidery thread for bobbin-work should be relaxing and inspirational, not filled with frustration. If you have experienced problems using specialty threads —it snags, breaks, shreds, jams—it's time to take a second look and solve problems when they occur. Remember the basics—use quality thread, a proper needle, have a balanced tension (unless otherwise noted) and a lint-free machine.

When sewing with specialty threads, you may find yourself constantly changing and fine-tuning the machine's tension. That is normal since thread weights and textures are not the same as general sewing thread. Experiment with the upper tension—try bringing more bobbin thread up to the surface or drawing the upper thread more to the bottom of fabric. Some tension changes will create new and exciting effects, while some are essential to perfecting the simple satin stitch.

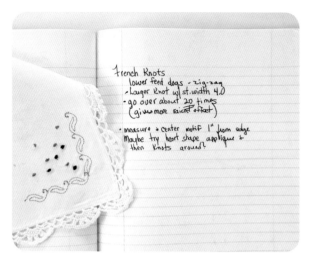

Test sew sample after sample, jotting down specifics for future reference.

TIPS AND TRICKS:

- Slow down! Try sewing at a slower speed. If your machine has speed adjustment, move to a slower speed.

- Check your needle. Is it the correct size and type to match fabric and thread (see chart on page 145)?

- Rethread the machine and make sure all threads pull through smoothly.

- Adjust tension settings. Always raise the presser foot when adjusting the tension.

- Try threads from different manufacturers. Amazingly, some will work better in your sewing machine than others.

- Test sew sample after sample, jotting down specifics for future reference.

sewing 101

Practice with specialty threads and decorative stitching while making a crazy quilt wallhanging. Pull out those velvets and silks from your fabric stash and create a personal work of art. To make a crazy quilt, sew random fabric types, shapes and sizes onto a plain fabric foundation. Use your machine's built-in stitches to create fancy stitching and embellishments between the patches. Try metallic threads, add trims and laces—get creative!

trims

Add a professional, designer appearance to garments and sewing projects by adding trims. Trims are perfect to make hems crisp and adorn sleeves or waistbands. There is an enormous variety of trim available at both local sewing shops and through online retailers. You will find flat braids, gimp, petersham, fringe, soutache braid and even feathers in various types, textures and colors. Whether you want to add a subtle touch or are going bold with lots of color, there is certainly a trim for you! Try something new for your next project. With so many types and textures, how do you choose?

PRESHRINK TRIM

Choose trim to match the washing and drying care of your fabric. Before using gimp, braids or other trims, test shrinkage. Cut a 2" (5cm) length and measure it. Hand wash the trim in warm water. Don't twist to dry! Instead, place the trim flat on a towel and roll it up, squeezing out the excess water. If the finished project will be machine dried, place the test strip in a small lingerie bag and put in the dryer. It must be dried inside of a bag (even a pillow case works!) because putting the trim directly into the dryer will result in a tangled mess! Measure after washing and drying to determine the amount of shrinkage. If there's sufficient shrinkage, prewash all the trim before using.

CUT TRIM

When cutting trim for your sewing project, always cut at least 1" (2.5cm) more than you think you need. There is nothing worse than sewing trim on your "almost finished" project and discovering at the very end that you are short!

Preshrink a sample of your trim to determine if you need to preshrink all of your trim before sewing it onto the completed project.

GIMP

The term *gimp* has been around since the fifteenth or sixteenth century. At that time, trim was made from gimp thread, which was braided together to be used as narrow, decorative trim. Today, gimp can be made from silk, wool, rayon, knit or cotton thread. Some are made of heavy threads while others may have a wire running through them. Gimp can be found from ¼"–1½" (6.4mm–3.8cm) wide in a variety of colors and weaves. Gimp makes a perfect finishing trim for home décor items, jackets, curtains and dresses. Use it to cover seams, long hems or just add it where you want a burst of embellishment.

SEQUINS AND BEADS

Sequin and bead strips are timesavers when you need to sew row after row onto your project. Lots of care is needed to prevent unraveling and to prevent needle breakage while sewing. When beginning and ending a strip, it is best to remove the beads/sequins from the string, leaving a tail to tie off. This prevents accidental bulk or sewing over them with another seam.

Place a piece of tape onto the sequin or bead strip about 1" (2.5cm) beyond your ending point. Carefully remove at least ½" (12.7mm) of the sequins or beads by sliding them off the center thread. Using a hand needle, pull the thread tail to the backside of the project and tie off.

Gimp braid is available from plain and simple designs to intricate scrolls and patterns.

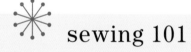

sewing 101

Petersham is 100 percent silk grosgrain, available in a variety of widths from 6mm–50mm.

Place a piece of tape onto the sequin or bead strip about 1" (2.5cm) beyond your ending point.

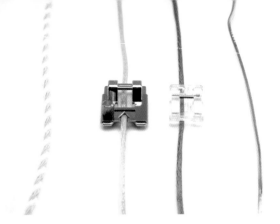

Rounded braids require a foot with a groove under-neath to accommodate the shape.

BRAID

Braid is made from intertwining yarns made of rayon, cotton, silk, chenille or even leather. Flat braids and rickrack tend to fray when cut. If possible, add them so the raw ends fall into an enclosed seam. If adding to readymade clothes, satin stitch the ends, turn the ends under and topstitch in place, or singe the ends of synthetic braid. Use caution when sewing after singeing as it leaves a plastic chunk that will break the needle.

Rounded braids require a foot with a groove under-neath to accommodate the shape. Some feet have a groove underneath the center of the foot, and others also have a thread guide. One strand of braiding can be placed in the groove.

 sewing 101

When sewing several strands of narrow braid simultaneously, use a cording foot (see page 52). Each piece is held in place by a clip on top of the foot, and slid into a groove. Pull strands under and behind the foot to be sewn simultaneously with a zigzag or decorative stitch. Alternatively, a pin-tuck foot could be used for smaller cording by sliding each strand under a separate groove. If an appropriate foot is unavailable, place tape across the top of a wide presser foot. Puncture a hole in the center for the needle and feed trim under the tape.

Soutache Braid

Soutache braid is braid woven into a herringbone pattern around two strands of piping. It is typically used to make looped motifs. Pulling the piping helps form loops. Pull one side for loops in one direction, and the other for loops in the opposite. Pull at least 15" (38cm) before forming. Pin to a piece of foam while shaping.

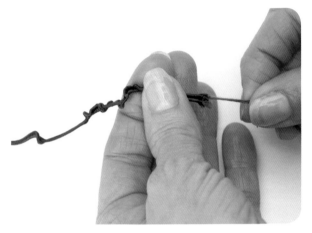

Pull one side of soutache braid to make a loop.

Pin soutache braid to foam board while forming.

Flat braid is available in a variety of widths and designs.

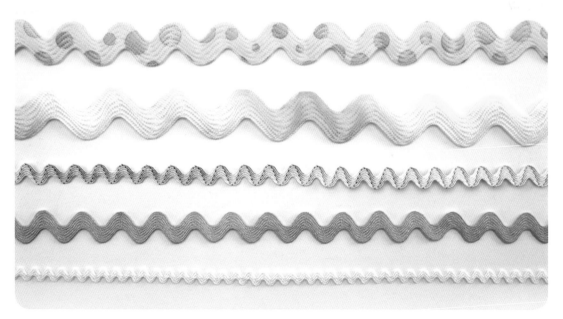

Rickrack comes in a variety of colors and in sizes from ⅛"–8½" (3.2mm–21.6cm).

embellishment techniques

Embellishments can include buttons, zippers, appliqué, piping, trim, threads, embroidery, sequins and other decorative and functional sewing notions. There are many techniques for sewing with these embellishments—some old and some new—that add interest and texture. Just a few examples are couching, passementerie, shirring and ribbon embroidery.

COUCHING

To *couch* means to stitch over cord. Trims, pearl cotton, braids and specialty threads can be sewn to the surface to add reinforcement, decoration or definition. Almost any material, from basic cording to elaborate metallics, can be suitable for couching. Add elegance with strands of beads, sequins, ribbons or strips of fabric. Choose a trim size according to design size. Smaller, tighter designs require smaller, flexible trims.

Choose the proper foot to aid in the couching process. If adding beads, choose a cording or braiding foot with a groove to aid in their smooth movement under the foot; for sequins use a sequin foot. Most ribbons, yarns, cording and threads can be couched with the zigzag presser foot or an open-toe foot for best visibility.

Stitches are an integral part of the couching design. Thread color affects how couching looks. Determine whether the stitches should be visible or blend in with the fabric. Matching the thread color to the cord color creates an appearance of being part of the fabric. Nylon monofilament thread gives the appearance that the trim is "floating" on the fabric. A more textured look is achieved when using metallic or heavy thread. The best bobbin thread for couching is 60 to 80 weight bobbin thread.

Almost any decorative stitch can be used to couch. A narrow zigzag, ladder stitch and other less dense stitches allow the cord to be prominent. Heavy, decorative stitches give cording a lesser role. Select a pattern and stitch width so that stitching falls on both sides of the trim, enclosing it completely.

COUCHING SETTINGS

Foot: Cordonnet, braiding, sequin, open-toe, embroidery, hemmer or cording

Needle: Appropriate for fabric and thread

Stitch: Straight, zigzag or decorative

Stitch length: 2mm–5mm

Stitch width: 0mm–5mm

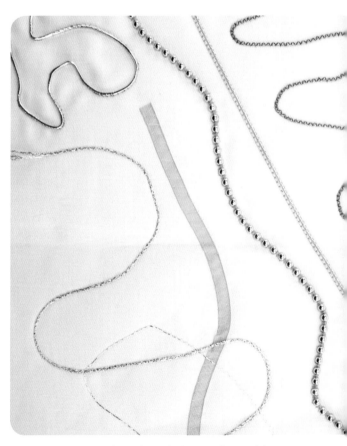

Various samples of couching designs and materials

124

Use a stabilizer appropriate for the fabric underneath to give a crisp, clean stitch and to prevent puckering and tunneling. Stabilizers provide the support for pucker-free couching. Choose a lightweight interfacing for cottons, silks, knits and polyester blends. If using fusible, fuse to wrong side of fabric. Another choice is tear-away stabilizer. Make the choice between fusible and nonfusible based on whether the fabric needs to have continual support long after many washings, or just needs the added support while couching. Wools, denims and other heavyweight fabrics are best couched with tear-away stabilizer to eliminate any added bulk.

When cutting the couching fabric, always cut larger than necessary. As the threads are sewn to the surface, the fabric pulls in, making it a smaller piece. After couching is completed, place the pattern piece on the embellished fabric and cut accordingly.

Couch over cording to create an interesting design.

Couching Methods

There are two methods of couching—following a marked design or free motion. If marking the fabric, transfer or draw a design on the right side of the base fabric. Remember, the more intricate the design, the narrower the couching trim you will use. Free-motion couching will result in a random design. Guide the cording with your hand in the directions you want to go. Using a free-motion foot and lowering the feed dogs is recommended.

Place one end of your cording at a raw edge to be sewn into a seam allowance or leave a 6" (15cm) tail at the beginning of the design to secure later. Place the trim under the foot. Using a zigzag or decorative stitch, sew over the trim so that the stitches encase the cord. A short stitch length will densely cover the cord, while a longer length will be more minimal. Leave another 6" (15cm) tail at the end.

If using water-soluble or tear-away stabilizer, remove it from the fabric. For couching that began and ended in the middle of fabric and not at a raw edge, thread a tapestry needle with the thread tails and draw to the back of fabric. Tie off. Lay the fabric with wrong-side-up on the ironing board and lightly press the trims. Never press hard enough to flatten.

Use a hemmer foot to couch over cording.

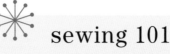

sewing 101

Try using the hemmer foot for couching. Twirl the cording into the scroll, pull it back under the foot and sew for a fast and easy alternative!

ELASTIC SHIRRING

There are several methods of sewing elastic shirring, but couching elastic cording provides you full control of how much gathering you want.

Elastic shirring can be made by couching elastic cord onto the wrong side of fabric in parallel rows. The number of rows is dependent on the width of shirring you want in your design. It can be added at the waist, around cuffs or near the neckline.

Mark the shirring rows on the wrong side of fabric, each about ⅜" (9.5mm) apart. Place the marked fabric wrong-side-up under the presser foot. Insert the cording under the foot on top of the fabric with at least 3" (8cm) behind the foot.

Select a zigzag stitch and adjust the stitch width so the stitches form over the cord, but never sew into it. Begin sewing, securing both beginning and ending stitches. Sew all subsequent rows carefully to keep them even and parallel.

After all the rows are completed, secure one side by sewing parallel to one raw edge over the cording. Pull the cording at the other end to gather.

Once gathered, secure the cording by sewing across the opposite edge. If additional embellishment is wanted, select a decorative stitch and sew on the right side over the shirred fabric. If the finished piece should remain "stretchy," do not add additional decorative stitching.

ELASTIC SHIRRING SETTINGS

Foot: Open-toe or embroidery

Needle: Appropriate for fabric

Stitch: Zigzag and decorative (optional)

Stitch length: 2mm–4mm

Stitch width: 2mm–2.5mm

Gather the elastic cording to create gathered piece.

Sew a decorative stitch over the elastic shirring if desired.

Couch elastic cording in parallel rows.

SMOCKING

Smocking is a series of parallel rows of gathered fabric secured with straight or decorative stitches. The honeycomb stitch results in small diamond-shaped smocking, while a motif stitch lends an embroidered appearance.

Smocking draws the fabric up a considerable amount, so the smocking must be completed before cutting the final pattern pieces. To cut your fabric before smocking, place the pattern pieces on the fabric following the pattern layout. Leave at least 6" (15cm) of room around all sides of each piece that will be smocked.

To begin smocking, set the straight stitch length to 3mm–5mm and loosen the upper tension. Baste across

SMOCKING SETTINGS

Foot: Open-toe, gathering, edgestitch

Needle: Appropriate for fabric

Stitch: Straight and decorative (optional)

Stitch length: 3mm–5mm (basting)

Stitch width: 0mm

the fabric, leaving long thread tails at the beginning and end. Don't backtack. Sew parallel rows about ⅜" (9.5mm) apart.

Pull the bobbin threads to gather the desired amount. Smooth gathers by lightly pressing. Select a decorative stitch. For very lightweight fabrics, place a narrow strip of fabric directly under the line of gathering for additional support. Sew the decorative stitch in between the basting lines. Remove the basting threads.

Once smocking is completed, finish the pattern cutting. Place the pattern on the smocked piece, aligning the smocking as desired and cut using the pattern instructions.

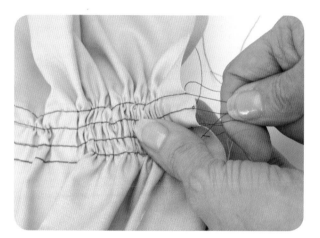

Pull bobbin threads to gather the desired amount.

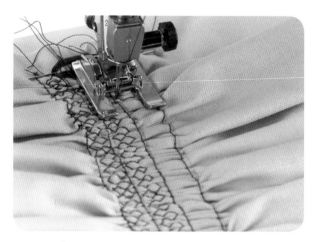

Sew a decorative stitch in between the basting lines.

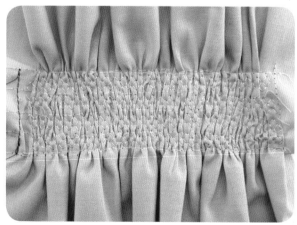

Remove the basting threads to complete the smocking (back of piece shown).

PASSEMENTERIE

The term *passementerie* can refer to the trim or to the process of embellishing with trim or cording. Typically, passementerie trim is made by sewing braids together to create one strip of elaborately embellished trim. You can easily create passementerie to match your sewing project by combining several trim types.

Make Passementerie Trim

Find and mark the center of your base trim. This is the trim the other trims will be sewn onto.

- **Using 2–3 trims:** Select a base trim that is at least two times as wide as the second trim. Sew the second, and more elaborately embellished trim directly down the center of the base trim. If desired, sew a third trim directly onto the second trim.

- **Using 4 trims:** Select a base trim that is at least two times as wide as the other trims. Center the first trim on the base with one edge directly on the center line. Center the second trim on the base on the other side of the center line. Sew these trims in place. Sew a fourth strip on top of the previous trims, directly down the center.

PASSAMENTERIE SETTINGS

Foot: Open-toe, braiding, cording

Needle: Appropriate for fabric and braid

Stitch: Straight

Stitch length: 2.5mm–4mm

Stitch width: 0mm

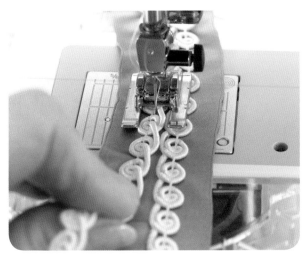

Using three trims: Sew two strips down the center.

Using four trims: Sew a fourth strip on top of the previous trims, directly down the center.

Various samples of passementerie

Passementerie as Embellishment

The term *passementerie* also suggests embellishing with trim or cording to create a design on fabric. You can use a commercially prepared design or easily create your own to suit the project. Swirls and scrolls work very well with passementerie. When possible, begin and end so that the raw edge of the trim will later be sewn into a seam. If that's not possible, leave a 6" (15cm) tail at both the beginning and end. With a large needle, pull the ends through to the back of the fabric and tie off.

Draw a design on the right side of the fabric with a removable marking pencil. Back the fabric with stabilizer. Attach a cording foot or an open-toe foot for wide visibility, and set the machine to a straight stitch. Place cording under the foot in the correct groove, and pull it several inches behind the foot. Check to ensure the needle falls in the center of the trim. Begin sewing, following the design with the cording. Sew slowly around curves as the braid may tend to slide to the side of the hole. Raise and lower the presser foot as you pivot.

Twin needles can be used to sew both sides of ribbon or braid simultaneously. Insert a twin needle and select a straight stitch. Set a stitch width of 2.5mm–3.5mm, determined by the width of the trim. If the trim is wider than the groove underneath the cording foot, choose a different but appropriate foot.

Stitch down the center of the trim.

sewing 101

No need to limit passementerie to garments. Utilize the lovely trims on furniture and drapery, such as fluffy fringe, tassels trimmed with sparkling crystals or silk cording. Be creative!

BOBBIN WORK

Sewing upside-down produces some interesting results. Add texture to your projects with a technique called *bobbin work* (also called *reverse bobbin work*). Stitching is done with heavy thread, cord or yarn, such as pearl cotton, pearl crown rayon, silk ribbon, ribbon floss, wooly nylon, baby yarn or other thick decorative threads wound on the bobbin. Sewing is done upside-down with the bottom becoming the right side when finished. In this technique, the bobbin thread is much heavier than the top thread, so adjustments will need to be made to the bobbin tension, or in some cases, bypassed entirely. The looser the bobbin tension, the "loopier" the stitches will be. Adjust to achieve the texture and effect you want.

Wind the bobbin slowly or by hand with any of the cords or yarns mentioned above. Since the fiber for bobbin work is thicker than regular thread, it takes up more space on the bobbin, so wind at least two or three bobbins to save time while sewing. The thread needs to flow smoothly off the bobbin, so you will need to either adjust the bobbin tension or bypass the tension slot in the bobbin case. If you need to bypass the bobbin tension, place the bobbin in the bobbin case but don't pull the thread through the tension slot. It will still turn the bobbin counterclockwise, although not in the bobbin tension. Many machines won't need to bypass the bobbin tension, with adjustments made to the bobbin tension. Check your manual or dealer for specific instructions for your machine if you are unsure.

sewing 101

Always make bobbin tension changes in quarter turns, making it easier to return to the original position. Purchase a secondary bobbin case dedicated to bobbin work to eliminate tension changes for regular sewing.

BOBBIN WORK SETTINGS

Foot: Open-toe, embroidery or free-motion

Needle: Appropriate for fabric and thread

Stitch: Straight or decorative

Stitch length: 3.0mm–5mm

Stitch width: 0mm

Note: *If using a free-motion foot, lower your feed dogs.*

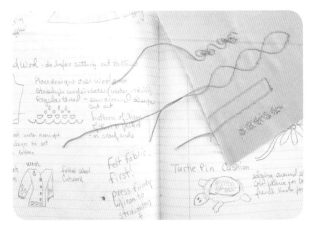

Jotting notes in a sewing journal makes for quick and easy reference later. It's especially helpful to record your methods for working with specialty thread or new techniques.

Finished bobbin work piece

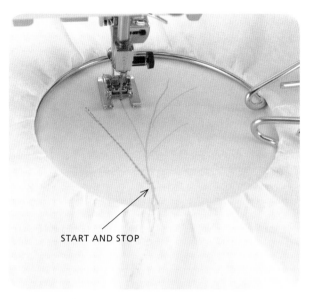

START AND STOP

Sew your design in one continual motion or pass, starting and stopping at the same place. This adds texture and eliminates too many thread tails in your design.

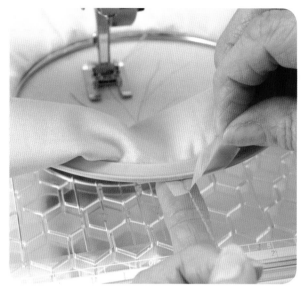

Tape the thread tail out of the way to keep it from becoming embedded as you sew.

Always test stitch a sample and make adjustments as necessary. The straight stitch may work beautifully, but a decorative stitch may require a tension adjustment. The bobbin threads should lie flat on the fabric. If stitches are loose, increase the upper tension.

Use an embroidery or satin foot for more controlled designs or a free-motion foot for free motion and intricate curves. A foot with a groove underneath allows the dense stitches to move smoothly under the foot.

The choice of which stitch to use is your personal choice. Straight stitches are often the best due to the heavy thread. Very short stitches may create thread jams, so choose a longer stitch if necessary; final stitch length is dependent on fabric weight and ribbon size. The upper thread will be the bottom stitches, so choose color accordingly. Invisible or matching upper thread will disappear into the design.

A lightweight stabilizer can be used, with the design drawn on the right side. The type of stabilizer is dependent on the type of project. If the fabric needs continued support, choose a stabilizer that will remain after washing. If support is not necessary, choose a wash-away stabilizer. Draw the design directly onto the stabilizer, not the fabric.

If sewing on a very lightweight fabric, a hoop may be necessary. Hoop the fabric with the right side of the fabric against the the outer hoop. The right side of the fabric will lie on the machine bed, and the drawn design will face up. If working with a free-motion foot, cover or lower the feed dogs.

Take one stitch and then hold the bobbin thread out of the way. If desired, tape the thread tail out of the way to keep it from becoming embedded as you sew. Leave a sufficient thread tail to later pull to the wrong side and tie off. (You will need to do this every time you change threads.)

Sew slowly around the traced design. As you sew, always remember that the finished design will be underneath—what you see as you sew will be the back. The best stitching occurs by moving the hoop slowly and at a consistent speed.

When finished, leave a long thread tail. Remove the hoop from under the foot. Use a large embroidery or tapestry needle to pull all thread tails to the wrong side and tie off.

SILK RIBBON EMBROIDERY

Embroider with your sewing machine using 2mm or 4mm silk ribbon. Hand wind the ribbon onto the bobbin, or wind it slowly on the sewing machine. Keep the ribbon flat as it winds. Place the bobbin in the bobbin case and loosen the tension until the ribbon pulls out smoothly. Check your machine manual—it may suggest bypassing the bobbin tension entirely. Use monofilament (invisible) thread or matching color for the top thread. Increase the upper tension to 8–9. Use an embroidery foot or free-motion foot (lower or cover feed dogs for free-motion embroidery).

Draw or transfer your design to the wrong side of the fabric. Place water-soluble stabilizer on the top and bottom of the fabric, and hoop.

Take one stitch and draw up the silk ribbon to the top. A heavy tapestry needle may be necessary. Leave a 4" (10cm) tail at the beginning and ending. Slowly stitch the design. Use a large needle to draw the tails to the wrong side, and tie off to finish.

SILK RIBBON EMBROIDERY SETTINGS

Foot: Free-motion, open-toe or embroidery

Needle: Appropriate for ribbon size

Stitch: Straight

Stitch length: Varies

Stitch width: 0mm

Note: *If using a free-motion foot, lower your feed dogs.*

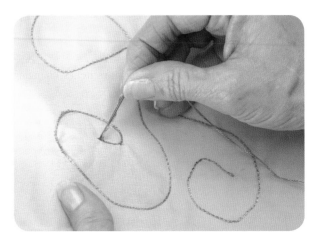

Use a large needle to draw the tails to the wrong side, and tie off to finish.

FRENCH KNOTS

Want to add more texture and interesting features to your project? Add a few French knots here and there. To create machine stitched French knots, cover or lower the feed dogs. Take a couple of straight stitches in place to secure. Use a zigzag stitch, with a width determined by the desired size of the French knot. Sew about ten zigzag stitches in place until the desired height is achieved. Sew several straight stitches in place to secure. Pull threads to the wrong side and tie off. The heavier the thread, the thicker and more prominent the knots.

Finished French knots

THREAD WORK

Want to try *painting* with your sewing machine and some lovely thread? Follow a design in the fabric, create your own design or design as you go! Thread sketching and thread painting are achieved using needle and specialty threads, alomg with the machine's zigzag and straight stitches. Stitch like you're using a pencil to follow the design. Thread painting has filled-in stitches, whereas thread sketching is similar to an outlined drawing.

Draw or transfer your design to the top of the fabric. Place stabilizer underneath the fabric to prevent puckering of the dense stitching. Take one stitch and draw the bobbin thread to the surface. While holding both threads behind the foot, sew three or four securing stitches. Trim tails. Outline and fill in the design with stitches, changing thread colors as desired. When finished, take several securing stitches. Trim thread tails close to the fabric.

THREAD WORK SETTINGS

Foot: Free-motion, open-toe or embroidery

Needle: Appropriate for fabric and thread

Stitch: Straight and zigzag

Stitch length: Varies

Stitch width: Varies

Note: *If using a free-motion foot, lower your feed dogs.*

TIPS AND TRICKS:

• Straight stitches are best for outlines and accents.

• Zigzag stitches are used for filling in the design.

• When using a zigzag stitch, move the hoop in a forward and backward motion to fill the design area.

• Sew at a constant speed to achieve even stitches.

• Outline and fill in areas beginning at the bottom of the design.

• Sew multiple stitching rows side by side while following the shape of the design.

• Change color and add hues by stitching part of the design with some jagged edges, and continuing the design with a different color.

• Dark colors work well as accent stitching.

Draw or transfer your design to the top of the fabric.

Change color and add hues by stitching part of the design with some jagged edges, and continuing the design with a different color.

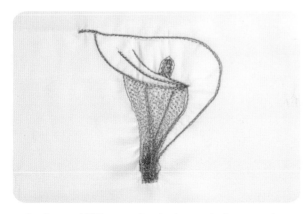

Outline and fill in areas beginning at the bottom of the design.

FRINGE

Add fringe to the fabric's edge using the tailor tack (fringe) foot and the zigzag or ladder stitch. The fringe foot has a raised metal bar; stitches are formed over this bar to make thread loops necessary for fringe. Designs with large curves or straight lines are best due to the nature of the foot.

To prevent threads from tangling in the bobbin area, place wash-away stabilizer directly under the edge of fabric that will be fringed. One stitch should fall onto the fabric edge and the other should fall onto the stabilizer.

Sew fringe to the edge of the project.

FRINGE SETTINGS

Foot: Tailor tack (fringe) and zigzag or embroidery

Needle: Appropriate for fabric and thread

Stitch: Zigzag, ladder stitch

Stitch length: 2.5mm–4mm

Stitch width: 3mm–5mm (adjust according to foot and desired length of fringe)

Select the desired stitch, reduce the upper tension, and set a stitch width of 3mm–5mm. At the beginning and ending of each row, secure with several straight stitches.

To secure the fringe stitches, attach an embroidery or zigzag foot. Adjust the stitch width from 2mm–3.5mm. Satin stitch along the fabric edge to secure the stitches. The bobbin thread will draw to the very edge of the fringe and can be removed or left intact. When finished, soak in warm water to rinse out the stabilizer.

FAUX CHENILLE

Faux chenille provides texture and interest to fabric. Use the tailor tack (fringe) foot and heavy thread. Mark a design on the fabric with a fabric marking pen. Designs with wide curves or straight lines work best with the fringe foot. The heavier the thread, the thicker the fringe. Typical thread size to use is 30 or 40 weight.

Place stabilizer under the fabric and adjust the stitch width to 2mm. Make sure the needle clears the raised metal bar. Begin sewing, following the design. Secure beginning and ending stitches with a straight stitch.

Sew rows close together to create faux chenille.

FAUX CHENILLE SETTINGS

Foot: Tailor tack (fringe)

Needle: Appropriate for fabric and thread

Stitch: Zigzag

Stitch length: Varies

Stitch width: 2mm–5mm

When each row is completed, slide the fringe off the back of the bar. Lower the foot and begin a new row. While sewing each new row, gently flatten previous loops with your fingers to keep them from entangling with the row being sewn. Each new row is sewn close to the last. If sewing curves, gently ease threads off the back of the foot while sewing.

When finished, leave a 2" (5cm) tail. Pull threads to the wrong side of the fabric and tie off. Or set the stitch width to 0mm and take several beginning and ending securing stitches.

BATTENBERG LACE

Battenberg lace was very popular during the 1930s and 1940s. As early as the seventeenth century, Battenberg lace was made by hand. Achieve similar results by using decorative stitch patterns on the machine and Battenberg tape. Battenberg tape is available as straight edge (two straight edges) and picot-edge (one straight and one picot edge).

Vintage Battenberg tape needs to be gathered to fit around curves, but newer tapes are much easier to use. The straight edges of newer Battenberg lace have a heavy cord running along the edges. To shape the tape around curves, pull this cord to gather the lace. The side you pull depends on the direction of the finished curve.

To begin, draw or transfer your design to thin paper, woven stabilizer or pattern tracing material. Place a water-soluble stabilizer over the design, and pin both layers to a piece of foam board to hold it taut and in place.

Find the heavy cord at the edge of Battenberg tape and pull out about 20" (51cm), gathering all but the first several inches. The curves should lay flat. Designs with only inside curves are shaped by pulling the thicker cord from one edge. Those with inside and outside curves should have the cord gathered on both edges.

(continued on next page...)

BATTENBERG LACE SETTINGS

Foot: Free-motion, embroidery, open-toe, zigzag

Needle: Microtex 80/12

Stitch: Straight and zigzag

Stitch length: 1.5mm–2.5mm

Stitch width: 0mm–1.5mm

Note: *If using a free-motion foot, lower your feed dogs.*

Pin the traced design covered with stabilizer onto a foam board.

To shape the tape around curves, pull the cord to gather the lace.

Vintage piece of Battenberg lace

(Battenberg Lace continued...)

Begin forming the tape around the design, pinning it through the stabilizer and into the foam board. Ease and shape the tape into curves so it lays flat following the design. Gently manipulate the gathered tape to fall smoothly around curves while still remaining flat. As you complete sections of the design, begin removing pins and secure the tape to the stabilizer with a fabric glue stick. Continue working in small sections until the design is complete. At the beginning and ending of the tape, place the raw edge under another section of tape, or fold the raw edges under and secure with glue.

Gently manipulate the gathered tape to fall smoothly around curves while still remaining flat.

Anywhere the tape crosses, sew two to three straight stitches in a zigzag motion.

sewing 101

Temporary glue adhesive is washable and will not gum up your machine's needle.

Attach an open-toe, embroidery or zigzag foot for best visability. Lower or disengage the feed dogs and insert a Microtex 80/12 needle (works best when sewing through water-soluble stabilizer). For the best results, use 50 or 60 weight embroidery thread matching the color of the Battenberg tape.

Carefully remove the stabilizer layer with the lace on top from the board. Stitch around the outer edges of the tape with a straight basting stitch, sewing through the stabilizer. Anywhere the tape crosses, sew two to three straight stitches in a zigzag motion, or use a small zigzag stitch (stitch width 1.8mm, stitch length 1.8mm).

Next, using 30 weight matching embroidery thread, sew filler stitches in each opening to add embellishment and stability. Fill each open area with your choice of bars or a combination of bar stitches.

TYPES OF FILLER STITCHES:

- **Richelieu bars:** Mark placement dots on opposite sides of the opening using water-soluble marking pen. Stitch in place several times on one dot to secure. Stitch to the opposite dot and back at least three times to make cords (each right next to the previous). Select a small zigzag stitch and couch over the bars, moving slowly to ensure coverage. Repeat for each Richelieu bar, and secure stitching on the last one.

- **Gridwork:** Stitch as for Richelieu bars. Then stitch perpendicular rows in the opposite direction.

- **Spiderweb or windmill:** Mark the top and bottom of the opening, and mark each side of the opening in quarters. Secure stitches at one of the points along the opening. Stitch to the opposite side with a long, straight stitch. Change to a narrow zigzag and stitch back over the filler cord just prepared. Repeat for remaining rows, moving in a spiderweb formation, always using the narrow zigzag to stitch back over the filler cord.

Richelieu bars: Stitch to the opposite side and back.

Gridwork filler stitches

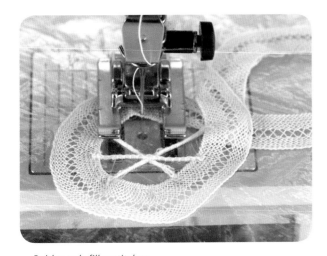

Spiderweb filler stitches

Remove the lace from the hoop. Cut and tear away excess stabilizer very carefully and rinse in cool water, soaking about five minutes. Iron the lace using a medium cotton setting.

Once completed, Battenberg lace can be sewn to garments, table runners or napkin edges. Determine the placement and pin the lace to the fabric. Attach a regular presser foot and select a narrow zigzag stitch. Sew the lace to the fabric along the edge of the lace. Cut away the fabric under the lace using appliqué or embroidery scissors.

For added embellishment and texture, tulle or netting can be placed in between the water-soluble stabilizer and the lace. Where the stabilizer will wash away, the tulle and netting will remain under the filler stitches. For this, layer water-soluble stabilizer, tulle/netting and Battenberg lace, and follow as previously instructed.

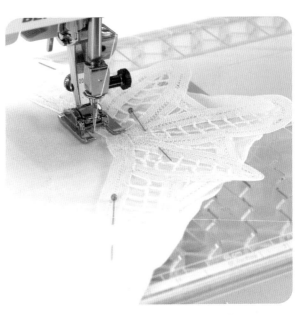

Sew the lace to the fabric along the edge of the lace.

BASIC APPLIQUÉ

Appliqué is the technique of sewing one fabric shape onto a background fabric. Appliqué pieces are typically stitched with satin stitches, but other stitch patterns can be used to alter and enhance the design. Dense stitches, such as satin stitches, are best for covering raw edges. Use a stitch width of 2mm–5mm and a stitch length of 0.5mm or less. Small, detailed appliqué pieces are easier to manage with a narrow stitch width. Appliqué pieces with finished edges, such as grosgrain ribbon or turned-under edges, can be sewn using stitches that are more open. Experiment using the blanket stitch, Parisian hemstitch, picot, a shortened blind stitch or a stretch blindstitch.

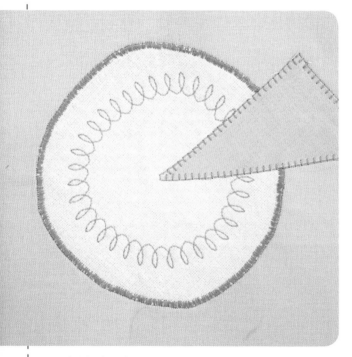

Finished appliqué piece

BASIC APPLIQUÉ SETTINGS

Foot: Open-toe or embroidery

Needle: Appropriate for fabric

Stitch: Zigzag or decorative

Stitch length: 0mm–1mm

Stitch width: 2mm–5mm

APPLIQUÉ TIPS:

- Loosen the upper tension slightly so the top thread pulls to the bottom, creating smooth, even satin stitches.

- Use stabilizer to prevent puckering and tunneling.

- Use a zigzag or appliqué foot, which has a wedge-shaped indentation on the sole to allow dense stitches to move freely under the foot. An edgestitch foot with a metal guide is also appropriate—the guide helps align the appliqué edge with the stitches.

- Fusible web products or temporary spray adhesives save time by holding appliqué pieces until stitched. Most temporary spray adhesives disappear within a few days.

- Appliqué pins are the best choice for holding pattern pieces in place because they are shorter than normal pins. Clear tape also works!

sewing 101

Need a quick stabilizer for appliqué? Save used dryer sheets and use them in place of purchased stabilizer.

CORDED APPLIQUÉ

Add interest and texture to appliqué by adding cording, such as pearl cotton, crochet thread or buttonhole twist, around the edges. To keep the cording directly under the needle, use a cording foot. For thick cord, choose a foot with a groove underneath so stitches flow smoothly. If your foot has a hole, run the cord up through it to keep cording directly under the needle.

Always adjust the stitch width to encase the cording. Leave a thread tail of at least 6" (15cm) at the beginning and end. If using thin cord, pull the tails to the back of the fabric and tie off. When using thick cording, butt the ends together and finish the stitchiing.

CORDED APPLIQUÉ SETTINGS

Foot: Braiding, cording, open-toe or embroidery

Needle: Appropriate for fabric

Stitch: Zigzag, satin

Stitch length: 2.5mm–3mm

Stitch width: 2mm–5mm

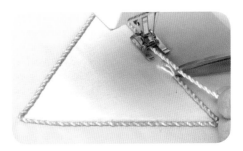

When using thick cording, butt the ends together, cut off excess and finish the satin stitch.

TRANSPARENT APPLIQUÉ

Transparent appliqué is achieved by layering sheer fabric underneath background fabric, instead of cutting individual appliqué pieces and sewing in the traditional manner. Many lovely effects can be achieved, with some appearing like cutwork.

Use fabrics such as organza, organdy, silk and chiffon. To add more depth to your finished appliqué, layer multiple pieces or colors of sheer fabrics.

Mark the appliqué design on tear-away stabilizer, and place it on the wrong side of the sheer fabric. Place the sheer fabric onto the wrong side of the background fabric. With wrong-side-up, begin outlining the appliqué design on the tear-away stabilizer using a straight stitch. Turn to the right side of the background fabric and cut away all background fabric inside the stitched shape, trimming close to the stitching line. Working from the right side, satin stitch around the raw edges. Remove the tear-away stabilizer. Turn to the wrong side and trim excess sheer fabric close to the satin stitches.

TRANSPARENT APPLIQUÉ SETTINGS

Foot: Open-toe or embroidery

Needle: Appropriate for fabric and thread

Stitch: Satin, blanket or straight

Stitch length: 0mm–3mm

Stitch width: 2mm–3mm

Layer the sheer appliqué fabric underneath the background fabric.

Finished transparent appliqué piece

REVERSE APPLIQUÉ

Fusing appliqué pieces creates sharp edges and reduces puckering. However, there are many types of fabric that are lovely as appliqué but can't be fused. Try reverse appliqué! The appliqué pieces aren't initially cut out, so using this technique eliminates frayed edges when using sheer fabrics or even delicate lace.

Cut your appliqué base fabric several inches larger than the dimensions of the finished design. Place the appliqué fabric right-side-up on the right side of the background fabric. Mark the design on tear-away stabilizer and place it on the wrong side of the background fabric. With the wrong side up, straight stitch around the design. Turn to the right side and trim the appliqué fabric outside of the stitching lines, trimming close to the stitching. Satin stitch from the right side to cover all raw edges.

Don't stop with using only fabrics for appliqué! Experiment with mylar embroidery film, fantasy film or Angelina fibers to add sparkle and shimmer to your projects. Each is available in a variety of colors. Some of the film and fibers are washable, but always check before beginning the sewing project.

When working with embroidery film and Angelina fibers, take advantage of all your machine's decorative stitches to provide interest and texture. Place the film on the right side of the fabric and sew a design on top with a straight stitch. Add decorative stitching at ⅛" (3.2mm) intervals to loosely cover the film. Trim (or tear away) excess film. Satin stitch over the raw edges.

Try this appliqué method and these mediums with your embroidery machine, too!

sewing 101

Angelina fibers are designed to fuse to each other with a low heat iron. Always place a pressing cloth on top of the fibers when ironing.

REVERSE APPLIQUÉ SETTINGS

Foot: Open-toe, embroidery or zigzag

Needle: Appropriate for fabric

Stitch: Straight or satin

Stitch length: 0mm–1mm

Stitch width: 2mm–3mm

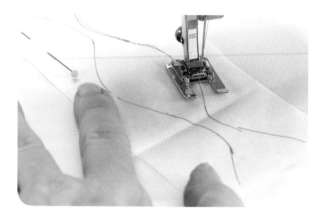

With the wrong side up, straight stitch around the design.

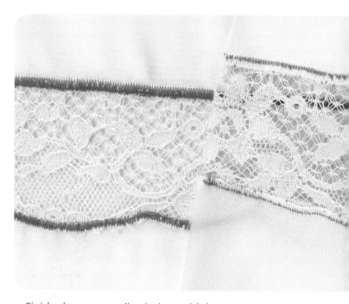

Finished reverse appliqué piece with lace

PERFECT SATIN STITCHES

Appearance is everything! Satin stitching is appropriate for decorative stitching, edgings and outlines. Use lightweight bobbin thread and decrease the upper tension so upper threads show on the wrong side. Guide satin stitches perfectly around corners, through curves, and keep those inside points sharp. When approaching corners and points, think about where the needle will fall and where the next stitch begins. Lower the needle and pivot accordingly.

- **Curves:** Sew slowly and pivot the fabric frequently with the needle down at the outside edge of the stitch.

- **Inside corners:** Stitch past the corner a distance equal to the width of the satin stitch. Stop with needle down on the left swing of stitching; raise presser foot. Pivot and stitch the next side.

- **Outside corners:** Take one stitch past the corner, stop with the needle down on the right swing of stitching. Raise the presser foot, pivot and satin stitch the next side.

- **Inside points:** Stitch past the point a distance equal to the width of the satin stitch. Stop with the needle down at the inner edge of stitching. Raise the presser foot and pivot 90 degrees. Take two to three stitches. Stop

SATIN STITCH SETTINGS

Foot: Open-toe, embroidery or zigzag

Needle: Appropriate for fabric

Stitch: Satin

Stitch length: 0mm

Stitch width: 2mm–3mm

with the needle down on the inner edge and raise the presser foot. Pivot the fabric and stitch next side.

- **Outside points:** Stitch past the point, stopping with the needle down at the outer edge of the stitching. Raise the presser foot and pivot 90 degrees. Take two to three stitches. Stop with the needle down on the outer edge of stitching. Raise the presser foot, pivot the fabric and stitch the next side.

- **Tapered outside points:** Stitch, stopping when the inner edge of the stitching meets the other side of the tapered point. Raise the presser foot and pivot just slightly. Stitch, gradually narrowing the stitch width to 0. Stop at the point. Raise the presser foot and pivot the fabric. Begin stitching, gradually widening the stitch width to the original width.

Curve—slowly pivot

Inside corner after pivot

Inside point ready to pivot

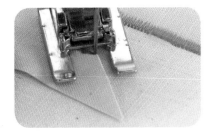

Inside point after pivot

Approaching outside corner

Tapering down to 0 width

DOUBLE AND TRIPLE PIPING

Add a single, double or triple piping strip to garments or home décor projects. The size of the cording used depends on the project and the fabric weight. Add tiny triple piping to sleeves or along a blouse front. Grab the jumbo cording and make a bold statement on pillows.

For double piping, cut two strips of cording the desired length. Cut the fabric into bias strips 1¾"–2" (4.4cm–5.1cm) wide for a final ⅝" (15.9mm) seam. The fabric strip should be wide enough to fold over the cording and allow for the ⅝" (15.9mm) seam allowance. Fold the fabric around the cording with wrong sides together. Position the cording to the left of the foot and adjust the needle position far left. Using a zipper foot, stitch close to cord. Adjust the foot or change the needle position so the stitches fall up to but not through the cording.

PIPING SETTINGS

Foot: Zipper

Needle: Appropriate for fabric

Stitch: Straight

Stitch length: 2.5mm–3mm

Stitch width: 0mm

For the second piping, cut a second fabric piece into bias strips 1½"–2" (3.8cm–5.1cm) wide. Fold around the second piece of cording, wrong sides together. Place this strip on top of the first piping, raw edges even. Stitch close to the cord, sewing through all layers.

For triple piping, cut the bias strips at least 2" (5.1cm) wide. Follow the directions for double piping, and then add a third. The piping is ready to be inserted into a seam.

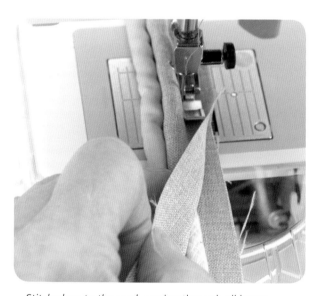

Stitch close to the cord, sewing through all layers.

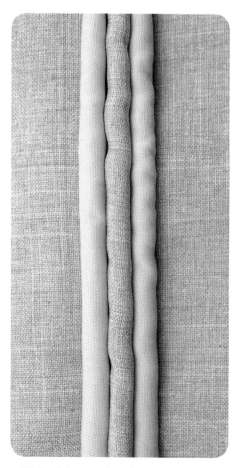

Triple piping, ready to be sewn into a seam.

SHIRRED PIPING

Shirred piping adds texture and interest to any sewing project. Add accents along edges or within seam allowances. For double and triple piping, cut a fabric strip wide enough to cover the cording plus additional 1¼" (3.2cm). Cut the length of fabric strip double the length of the cording.

Wrap the fabric around the cording, wrong sides together. Stitch across one end to secure. With the covered cording to the left of the needle, change the needle position to far left. Use a zipper foot to sew close to the cording but not through it. Stitch next to the cording. Sew 10" (25cm), stop with the needle in the fabric, lift the foot and pull the cording. The fabric will shirr behind the foot. Repeat until finished. When finished, sew across the end to secure. The shirred piping is ready to be sewn into a project. Try making double and triple shirred piping.

SHIRRED PIPING SETTINGS

Foot: Zipper

Needle: Appropriate for fabric

Stitch: Straight

Stitch length: 2.5mm–3mm

Stitch width: 0mm

Pull the cording and the fabric will shirr.

INSERTING PIPING INTO A SEAM

Properly inserting piping into a seam just takes a bit of practice. For best results, always begin at an inconspicuous point.

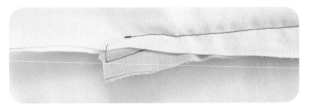

Angle the first piping end. Start stitching 1" (2.5cm) past this point.

Angle the second piping end, crossing over the first. Trim away the excess.

With raw edges together, pin one end of the piping to the fabric at an angle so the end of the piping extends past the seam allowance. Begin sewing the piping to the fabric about 1" (2.5cm) beyond this point.

Continue sewing the piping with a ⅝" (15.9mm) seam allowance. Stop several inches from the initial angled piping. Lower the needle to prevent the seam from moving. Gently angle the final end of the piping so it crosses the beginning angle. Pin it in place. Finish sewing the seam allowance, sewing slowly over the "hump" of the piping ends.

Completed joined piping

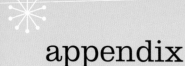

appendix

SEWING MACHINE PREVENTIVE MAINTENANCE

Regular cleaning and proper maintenance is key to preventing sewing problems and to keep the machine running smoothly. Keep the machine covered when not in use, change needles after eight hours of use, wind bobbins properly and clean the machine on a regular basis.

To clean the machine, lift the presser foot to release pressure between tension discs. Clean tension discs with folded piece of muslin (see page 44). Then spray compressed air from back to front to dislodge loose dirt and lint. Remove the needle, needle plate, bobbin, bobbin case and hook race (computerized machines won't have a removable hook). With a small brush, clean around and under the feed dogs. Spray the bobbin area with compressed air, spraying lint outward. Wipe the hook with a spot of oil on muslin. Clean inside the bobbin case with a lint brush and compressed air. Give the bobbin case a drop of oil before reinserting. Check manual for additional oiling spots of your machine. Replace with a new needle.

FABRIC WIDTHS

Standard fabric widths are 44"/45" (112cm/114cm) and 58"/60" (147cm/152cm), not including selvage. Fabric for quilt backings are 108"/110" (274cm/279cm) wide.

RUFFLING CONVERSION CHART

The standard rule is to cut the fabric 2.5 times longer than the finished piece.

FINISHED LENGTH	BEGINNING FABRIC LENGTH
18" (46cm)	45" (114cm)
24" (61cm)	60" (152cm)
30" (76cm)	75" (190cm)
36" (91cm)	90" (229cm)
40" (102cm)	100" (254cm)
44" (112cm)	110" (279cm)

STANDARD ZIPPER LENGTHS

Zippers are available in almost all sizes, with some being more commonly found. Specific zipper lengths can be found on the Internet and special ordered. This is certainly not an all-inclusive list.

TYPE	LENGTHS IN INCHES
Closed on one end	6"–23" (15cm–58cm)
Closed on both ends	6"–41" (15cm–104cm)
Open end—one way separating	9", 18", 26", 30" (23cm, 46cm, 66cm, 76cm)
Open on both ends—two way separating	22"–110" (56cm–279cm)
Coil-flat on one side, teeth on other	17", 30", 36", 60", 110" (43cm, 76cm, 91cm, 152cm, 279cm)
Invisible	10", 12", 14", 16", 18", 22", 24", 26" (25cm, 30cm, 36cm, 41cm, 46cm, 56cm, 61cm, 66cm)

THREAD AND NEEDLE CHART

FABRIC TYPE	THREAD TYPE	FABRICS	NEEDLE SIZE	NEEDLE TYPE
Light and delicate woven	Very fine cotton covered polyester, silk, lingerie, fine cotton (70/2, 80/2), mercerized cotton (50/2), polyester (100/2)	Chiffon, fine lace, organza, tulle, georgette, net, microfibers	60/8 to 70/10	Microtex, denim, universal
Lightweight woven	Silk, extra fine cotton-covered polyester, mercerized cotton (50/2, 50/3), polyester (100/3)	Batiste, crepe, chiffon, velvet, jersey, organdy, plastic covered, taffeta, voile, linen, lace, challis, chambray, eyelet, light polyesters and wools, charmeuse, dotted swiss	60/8 to 70/10	Microtex, denim, universal
Lightweight to medium-weight knits	Extra fine cotton-covered polyester, silk, mercerized cotton (50/2, 50/3), polyester (100/3)	Double knit, jersey, mesh, velvet, metallic, sweater, sweatshirt, fleece, velours, ribbed knits	60/8 to 80/12	Universal, stretch, ballpoint (size 65/9 for velvet)
Lightweight to medium-weight wovens	Polyester (100/3), cotton-covered polyester, mercerized cotton (50/2, 50/3)	Chambray, gingham, percale, metallic, seersucker, woven fabrics, broadcloth, linen, brocade, shantung, felt, felted fabric, polyester, woolens, acrylics, fleece, wools, gabardine, acrylics	60/8 to 90/14	Microtex, denim, universal
Medium to heavy-weight wovens	Cotton (50/3), cotton-covered polyester, polyester (100/3), quilting, jeans, topstitching, embroidery (40/3, 40/2)	Denim, drapery, gabardine, sailcloth, tweed, deep pile fabrics, brocade, corduroy, wool, wool blends, quilted	70/10 to 100/16	Microtex, denim, quilting, universal
Heavy wovens	Polyester (100/3), quilting, jeans, topstitching, embroidery (40/3, 40/2), button and carpet	Upholstery, heavy vinyl, coated fabrics, canvas, leather, duck, awning	80/12 to 100/16	Jeans, quilting, universal
Medium to heavyweight knits	Polyester (100/3), quilting, jeans, topstitching, embroidery (40/3, 40/2), vinyls use monofilament	Fur, fake fur, fleece, double knits	70/10 to 100/16	Jeans, quilting, universal
Specialty	Polyester (100/3), cotton-covered polyester, vinyls use monofilament	Ultrasuede, faux leather, vinyl, leather, fur, sherpa	65/9 to 100/16	Stretch, Microtex, jeans, universal, sharp wedge point (for leather)

STITCH PATTERNS

Stitch Types

Sewing machines can be straight stitch only, and others can have over four hundred built-in stitches. The stitches are known as utility, decorative, heirloom, quilting and buttonholes. Take a few minutes and identify some of them. Learning their various uses saves time while sewing and can help produce a well-sewn, long-lasting item. Your stitches may have different names than those listed here, but may produce the same or similar effects.

Utility Stitches

Take the time to locate stitch patterns on your machine. Some are called utility stitches since they are the most useful. Utility stitches take the chore out of sewing. Most manuals have a complete list of their stitches.

Reverse/Reinforcement Stitches

Reverse and reinforcement stitches are generally used at the beginning and the end of your sewing seam. These are also called *tacking stitches* and are a method of tying off your thread to prevent unraveling. Take about four tacking stitches in the same spot to secure your thread.

Find your reverse button. Older sewing machine models may have a lever. Whenever you push the reverse button or have the lever in the up position, the machine will sew in reverse.

STITCH	PATTERN	APPLICATION	STITCH WIDTH (MM)	STITCH LENGTH (MM)
Straight		All straight stitch and lockstitch work	Varies	Varies
Straight with adjustable needle positions		Sewing that requires different needle positions (zippers, piping, topstitching, etc.)	Varies	Varies
Zigzag		Overcasting, patchwork, and sewing appliqué	0.0mm–7.0mm	0.0mm–4.0mm
Multi-stitch zigzag (3 point)		Overcasting on medium-weight fabric, stretch fabric, darning, attaching elastic	1.5mm–7.0mm	0.2mm–4.0mm
Overcasting		Overcasting on lightweight and medium-weight fabrics	2.5mm–5.0mm	1.0mm–4.0mm
		Overcasting on heavyweight, thick fabrics	2.5mm–5.0mm	1.0mm–4.0mm
		Overcasting on heavyweight, thick fabrics	0.0mm–7.0mm	0.5mm–4.0mm
		Overcasting on stretch fabrics	0.0mm–7.0mm	0.5mm–4.0mm
Blind hem		Invisible hemming	Varies	Varies
Blind hem stretch		Hemming stretch fabric	Varies	Varies

SEWING WOVENS, KNITS AND SILKS CHARTS

WOVEN FABRIC	STITCH LENGTH (MM)	NOTES
Buttonhole	Preprogrammed when using buttonhole stitch	Match buttonhole to type of fabric and usage of buttonhole.
Shirts, blouses, tops	1.5mm–3.0mm	Lightweight: use 1.5mm–1.7mm; medium-weight: use 2.5mm–3.0mm
Children's garments	2.0mm–3.0mm	Finish raw edges to prevent fraying.
Dress shirt and tops	1.5mm–2.5mm	Smaller stitch length reduces the tendency to pucker.
Dresses and skirts	2.0mm–3.0mm	Or use a narrow zigzag.
Denim, jeans, jackets	3.0mm–3.5mm	Fewer stitches provide a contrast appearance when using heavier thread.
Pants, slacks, trousers	2.0mm–2.5mm	Lapped seams are durable side seams.
Twill pants and shorts	2.0mm–3.0mm	A longer stitch length minimizes puckering.

KNIT FABRIC	STITCH LENGTH (MM)	NOTES
Fleece	2.5mm–4.0mm	Use medium to long zigzag.
Dresses and shirts	2.0mm–2.5mm	Finer thread helps reduce puckering.
Infant wear	2.0mm–2.5mm	French seams are durable.
T-shirts, jersey tops	2.0mm–2.5mm	Zigzag stitch stretches with fabric.
Stretch knits—spandex and lycra	1.5mm–3.0mm	Use a zigzag or stretch stitch.
Swimwear	1.5mm–3.0mm	Use a small zigzag or stretch stitch.
Intimates and delicates	1.5mm–2.0mm	Use a fine needle and lingerie thread.

SILKS AND "LOOK-ALIKES"	STITCH LENGTH (MM)	NOTES
Silk	1.7mm–2.5mm	Fabric is cool in the summer, warm in the winter. If puckering occurs, shorten stitch length. Fairly wrinkle resistant.
Rayon	1.7mm–2.5mm	Wrinkles easily. Can build up static electricity.
Acetate	1.7mm–2.5mm	Drapes well, some blends are more wrinkle resistant.
Nylon	1.7mm–2.5mm	Very strong fabric.
Polyester	1.7mm–2.5mm	Wrinkle resistant. Holds more of a crease than others.

STABILIZER CHART

Each manufacturer has variations and additional specialty types, such as those for loose knits, denims or those that are soft next to the skin. Base your stabilizer choice on fabric and use.

When using stabilizer, spray the fabric with temporary basting spray to hold the fabric and stabilizer firmly together while sewing.

Stabilizers are usually available in white, black, beige, ivory and clear. They are available in rolls from 10"– 20" (25cm–51cm) wide and 5yd–22yd (4.5m–20m) long.

TYPE	CHARACTERISTICS	FABRICS AND USES	SUGGESTIONS
Cut-away	Doesn't degrade when washed; available from light-to heavy-weight; trim excess after stitching; evenly woven with no stretch in any direction.	Stretch and loosely woven fabrics: knits, stretch, fleece, densely embroidered designs, satin stitching. Works well on decorative borders, sweatshirts, denim, crafts, and tote bags. Heavy weight provides firm base for bowls, hats, boxes.	Adhere to fabric before sewing with temporary basting spray.
Polymesh cut-away	Soft, yet strong sheer nylon; available in white and black, light- and medium-weight; doesn't show through to front—translucent quality makes it less visible under fabric.	Knits, lightweight, fleece, stretchy, sheer fabrics, 3D designs. Use as topper over metallic stitches. Also good for T-shirts and loose knits.	When hooping, don't stretch fabric.
Fusible fleece	Thick, lofty fabric, usually polyester; fusing on one side.	Creates loft in embroidered items. Use for crafts, totes, purses, wallets.	Take care when pressing as ironing can distort. Press—don't iron!
Tear-away	Stiff and paper-like; degrades over time and after washing; tears in all directions; available from light- to heavyweight.	Nonstretch, tightly woven fabrics, vinyl, leather.	If necessary, use more than one layer.
Adhesive tear-away	Two sheets bonded together—one adhesive and other is paper-like; also available as an iron-on with waxy coating on one side.	Knits, stretchy fabrics.	Don't use on terry cloth —will pull loops and may gum up the needle.
Water-soluble	Dissolves on contact with water; some brands are stable without stretching while others stretch and tear easily; available as film or mesh.	Very lightweight fabric. Use when both sides will show, such as cutwork, reverse appliqué and lace work. Use as a topping for looped and pile fabrics to prevent stitches from sinking into fabric.	Store in watertight bag, rinse in warm water, do not wring dry. May need several layers for sufficient support.
Water activated (tear- or cut-away)	Stays in place until glue is remoistened; available as cut-away or tear-away.	Lightweight, firmly woven bulky items.	The wetter it is, the stronger it holds fabric. Doesn't gum up needle. Patch small pieces to reuse.
Heat-away	Disintegrates into ashes with dry, hot iron; comes as fabric type resembling muslin or plastic film.	Use on all fabrics that withstand heat, cutwork and laces. Especially good for fabrics that cannot get wet.	Press with hot, dry iron and brush away residue.

TYPE	CHARACTERISTICS	FABRICS AND USES	SUGGESTIONS
Polymesh fusible	Sheer, lightweight nylon that can be fused with low iron setting.	Knits, lightweight, fleece, stretchy, sheer fabrics, 3-D designs. Use as topper over metallic stitches.	If hooping, don't stretch fabric.
Freezer paper	Adhered to fabric with medium iron setting.	Use as a replacement for tear-away when not available.	Dulls needles quickly.
Liquid starch	Mix with water to desired consistency; paint on with brush.	Use on lacy designs on washable fabrics.	Brush on, let dry, press and stitch. Or, dissolve scraps of water-soluble in water to create brush-on stabilizer.
Tulle and netting	Polyester netting in range of colors; continues support through repeated washings.	Use as topper to hold down pile on napped and pile fabrics.	Tear or trim away, match color to fabric and won't be seen.

INTERFACING CHART

TYPE	CHARACTERISTICS	FABRIC AND USES
Woven	Firm support, available as fusible and nonfusible; made from poly, cotton, rayon or blend; available as washable and/or dry clean.	Use in collars and shirt cuffs. Provides firm, crisp support.
Knit	Fusible; soft and drapes well; lightweight to heavyweight.	Use on light- to medium-weight fabrics.
Warp inserted knit	Knit fabrics with threads woven throughout; combines softness of knit and stability of woven; available in light- and medium-weights	Use in jackets, waistbands, coats. Provides structure without stiffness.
Stretch non-woven	Has high stretch.	Use on knit fabrics.
Nonwoven	Made from synthetic fibers; most common type of interfacing; available in various weights; fusible and nonfusible.	Use for minimal shrinkage. Best for medium- to heavyweight fabrics; use crosswise stretch for moderate shaping. Provides crispness.
Tricot-fusible	100 percent polyester, 60" (152cm) width; available in white, black, grey, ivory.	Can be used on lightweight woven fabrics. Provides soft support for knits.
Horsehair/canvas	Blend of wool and goat hair.	Provides crisp shaping for tailoring.
Double-sided fusible	Stiff and doesn't stretch or tear; fuses on both sides.	Use for purses, totes, bowls, 3-D crafts.
Translucent	Nonwoven, tear-away.	Use for foundation piecing, embroidery, dense stitching.
Paperless fusible	Brand name Mistyfuse; sheer and bonds when cooled; doesn't gum needles.	Use with all fabric weights, from delicates to velvets.

glossary

You will soon learn many more terms than those listed here, but these will provide a good starting point as you build your sewing vocabulary.

Adaptor: Used to change sewing feet easily. Attach the adaptor to your machine and push a lever in the back of the adaptor to attach and release various sewing feet.

Appliqué: Attaching one piece of fabric to another for decorative purposes, by sewing or fusing. Usually the satin stitch or blanket stitch are used, although other decorative stitches are easily adaptable.

Appliqué scissors: Used for cutting accuracy in many sewing and craft projects. They are distinguishable by having one blade that is similar to blades of regular scissors, while the second is flat, wider, and resembles the upper bill of a duck, offset for level cutting.

Awl: A sewing tool that has a sharp, round end and is used for poking holes in fabric, cutting the "keyhole" of the keyhole buttonhole, and for opening eyelets.

Backstitch: A backstitch is used at the beginning and ending of a seam to secure the threads. When piecing a quilt, the backstitch is not used since it adds bulk to the seam. Another term is *backtack*.

Ballpoint needle: Best needle for knit fabrics; the rounded tip does not pierce and damage the fabric.

Bar tack: Multiple, closely sewn zigzag stitches used at the end of buttonholes, or to tack a belt loop in place.

Baste: A stitch that temporarily holds fabrics together and is removed after permanent stitching is in place. The loose stitching is achieved by using the longest stitch length possible for the fabric. If the fabric gathers instead of lying flat, reduce the length of stitch.

Batiste: Fabric that is woven cotton or a blend. Comes in lightweight to medium-weight, and gives lovely hang to a garment. Used for hemstitching, making entredeux tape, baby garments and in sewing heirloom garments.

Batting: A cotton, wool, fiberfil or other blend with low, medium or high loft. It is sandwiched between fabrics for quilting, making a placemat, or any sewing project where you need some thickness. Another term is *wadding*.

Bead (buttonhole): Each side of a buttonhole.

Bias: The bias of a fabric runs diagonally at a 45 degree angle from the straight of grain. It is the diagonal intersection of the two fabric grains. Fabric cut on the bias will be very stretchy.

Bias tape: Bias tape is cut from the bias of the fabric, turned under, and pressed. Used for binding edges for stability or decorative purposes, especially when a bit of stretch is necessary for rounding curves. Bias tape can be made on the straight of grain if all edges to be bound are straight.

Binding: Encasing the raw edges of fabric with another fabric strip or bias tape.

Bird's nest: Tangles and knots on the wrong side of the fabric and in the bobbin area.

Blind hem: A blind hem is not seen on the front of the fabric and is nearly invisible. Only one piece of fabric thread is picked up, rather than a group of stitching. The hem is specially folded, and the guide of a blind hemmer foot maintains the left swing of the needle to catch only one fabric thread.

Blind stitch: Use the blind stitch and a blind hemmer to produce a nearly invisible hem on the front side of the fabric. (see *Blind hem*)

Bobbin: The bobbin holds the lower thread; as the needle penetrates the bobbin area, the thread forms a loop to make a stitch. Bobbins are placed in the bobbin case underneath the needle plate.

Bobbin case: Holds the bobbin and maintains tension on the lower thread. The bobbin case can be built in the machine (called a "drop-in" bobbin) or can be placed in the lower part of the machine.

Bodkin: Used to insert elastic, elastic cord or laces into a casing. Some have an eye at one end for threading cording or elastic. Others have a pincher which grabs the cording, helping you to insert it into casing.

Butting: Bringing the edges of two pieces of fabric together without any overlap.

Buttonhole: A slit in the fabric secured by stitching that allows a button to pass through. Can be made by hand or by machine.

Buttonhole cutter: A tool with a sharp, beveled edge. When pressed firmly in the center of a buttonhole, it opens the fabric without cutting into the stitching. A keyhole buttonhole cutter is also available. A seam ripper can also be used, although take great care not to cut the buttonhole stitches.

Carbon paper (dressmaker's): Use to transfer markings to fabric. Many can be brushed or rubbed off. Comes in yellow, green, white, blue and black. Choose a contrasting color to show markings easily. Don't iron over as it may remain permanently.

Casing: Folded fabric sewn to encase elastic, drawstrings or various cording.

Chalk (tailor's): Used to mark cutting notches, buttonholes, pleats and other pattern markings on fabric. Always check to ensure the marking chalk is removable and won't permanently damage the fabric.

Clip: Cutting a slash in the seam allowance, generally around curves so they lay flat without puckering.

Colorfast: Fabric is colorfast if the color/dye holds when washed, and doesn't bleed.

Cross tuck: Tucks stitched at 90 degree angles to each other. Sew straight tucks across the fabric, and then sew the second set of tucks at a 90 degree angle to the first set.

Crosswise grain: Made from threads woven perpendicular to the selvage. (see *Weft threads*)

Cutting line: The outermost line on a pattern showing where to cut.

Darn: To mend a hole in fabric using needle and thread, and crossing threads.

Dart: A tapered, V-shape sewn into the fabric to make an area smaller. Typically placed around the waistline, neckline or bust line for precise fitting.

Dress form: A headless, armless, legless form which gives a realistic, three-dimensional representation for fitting garments. Dress forms can be adjusted to specific body size and shape.

Ease (in patterns): Ease is an amount of space beyond actual body measurements in patterns to provide comfort. Ease is also a method of sewing one fabric onto a smaller size fabric without puckering or gathers.

Edgestitch: Sewing ⅛" (3.2mm) from a folded or seamed edge.

Embellish: Adding decorative stitching, cording, couching or other decorations to your sewing project.

Embroidery scissors: Used to cut embroidery threads, getting close to the embroidery but not cutting into it.

Emery bag: Used to sharpen and polish needles and pins, usually in the shape of a strawberry on a pin cushion. Best ones are filled with real emery grains.

Entredeux: A narrow strip of bastiste that has small holes running down the center, normally used in heirloom sewing. Can be purchased or created using a wing needle and an entredeux stitch on the sewing machine.

Eyelet: A small, round hole usually finished around the edges; used for passing cord and laces through.

Fabric width: The measurement of the fabric from selvage to selvage.

Facing: Sewn on the raw edge of the fabric and turned under to create a finished edge.

Feed dogs: The teeth under the needle plate that move the fabric while sewing.

Finger pressing: Using fingers to apply pressure to open a seam in fabric not suitable for an iron.

Finish (seam, edges): Prevents fraying of seams, can be turned under ⅛"–¼" (3.2mm–6.4mm) and sewn. Sew with an overcast or zigzag stitch, or serge.

Flat-felled seams: Provides a secure seam with all raw edges covered. Sew fabric wrong sides together, trim one seam allowance close to the stitching, turn the other seam allowance under to hide all raw edges, and stitch.

Fold line: The folded edge when fabric is folded lengthwise with selvage edges together. Some pattern pieces need to be placed "on the fold line" to avoid having a seam line.

Feet: Sewing machine attachments that attach to the needle bar. Each foot has a specific sewing purpose. For example, the sequins foot feeds strips of sequins through quite easily.

Frog: A decorative fastener made from looped and interwoven cording, sewn where the cords touch. They come in pairs, one part is a closure loop and the other is a raised knot to slip through the loop. An alternative to buttons or buttonholes. Can be purchased or you can create your own.

Fusible: Interfacing or stabilizer that is bound with heat. Has heat-activated residue on one side, and when ironed onto fabric is usually permanent.

Free motion: Moving the fabric in a freehand motion under the needle with the feed dogs down or covered.

Gather: Sewing parallel rows across the fabric using a basting stitch and pulling the two top threads to tighten the fabric around the thread.

Grain of fabric: The way the threads run in fabric. Grain can be either the lengthwise or crosswise threads in woven fabric. Pattern pieces are usually cut on the lengthwise grain to drape properly. Crosswise threads have more stretch than lengthwise. (see *Straight-of-grain, Weft threads, Warp threads*)

Gusset: A triangular shaped piece of fabric inserted into another fabric. Can provide additional movement in hemlines, sleeves, or be for decorative purposes only.

Ham (tailor's): A tightly stuffed curved pillow used as a mold when pressing curved areas of garments (such as sleeves).

Hem: A finished, turned-under edge on garments and sewing projects. A hem can be double or single folded. Double folded hems are folded twice and sewn. A single fold hem has a finished edge that is folded once and then sewn.

Hooks and eyes: A type of closure that has a hook on one side and an eye (loop) on the other. The hook slides into the eye to close the garment. Can sew on individually or use hook and eye tape.

Insertions: A strip of embroidered lace, entreduex or fabric placed between two other pieces. Usually for decorative purposes. Can insert entredeux between fabrics or between laces, for example.

Interfacing: Fabric used between fabric and facing to add body, strength and/or shape.

Interlining: Material used between two layers of fabric, usually the garment and the facing, to provide stability, strength and sometimes form.

Inverted pleats: Evenly spaced folds about 1" (2.5cm) apart that reverse the fold of the box pleat so the fullness is turned inward.

Iron: A heating tool used in sewing to press, and at times to straighten, fabric. A steamer iron will moisten the fabric, eliminate wrinkles and help set the press. Look for settings such as linen or cotton, and cooler settings for polyester and rayons. When sewing, match iron settings, with steam or without, to the type of fabric.

Ironing: Accomplished by moving the iron back and forth over fabric. Ironing is different from pressing used in sewing. (see *Pressing*)

Knife pleats: Series of folds formed by folding the fabric in the same direction, usually about 1" (2.5cm) apart.

Knots (French): A small decorative thread element made by wrapping thread around a needle several times and inserting into fabric, creating a raised knot. Can be sewn by machine by lowering feed dogs and repetitively stitching small zigzags in one spot.

Lapped seam: Seams that lay flat and are very strong. Sewn with two fabric pieces overlapping each other. Some have one fabric piece folded under for a finished look. Often used for leather, jeans and felting.

Layout: Placement of pattern pieces on the fabric, ready for cutting. If using a fabric with nap or print direction, use the *with nap* layout printed on the pattern.

Lengthwise grain: Threads that are continuous along the length of the fabric.

Lettuce hem: A finished frilled edge created by stretching the fabric while hemming. Works best on knits and sheer fabrics. Hemming on the bias creates more frills.

Lining: Fabric layer on the inside of some garments. Used to conceal seam construction, reduce wrinkling, and at times make it easier to get in and out of garments.

Loop turner: A long wire with a latch hook at one end used for turning fabric tubes, such as spaghetti straps and button loops.

Marking pencil: Sewing pencil used for drawing on fabric. Available in a variety of colors such as white, pink and blue. A brush removes marks. Always test fabric before using any marking pencil to ensure easy removal. It is not recommended to iron over the marks as they may become permanent.

Muslin fabric: Finely woven cotton blached or unbleached fabric. Available in a variety of sizes.

Nap: Napped fabrics, such as velvet and satin, reflect light differently depending on the direction they are cut. Napped fabrics may also have a one-way design. It is important to cut pattern pieces using the *with nap* pattern layout. (see *Layout*)

Narrow hem: Typically ⅛" (3.2mm) or ¼" (6.4mm) wide and used in lingerie, napkins, handkerchiefs, dress shirts and other items that need a tiny and less intrusive hem.

Needle: Long, slender tool with a pointed tip. Used to sew cloth using thread. Choose the sewing needle specific for the fabric, such as ballpoint for knits.

Nonwoven fabric: Fabric that is not woven or knitted. It is man-made and bonded with an adhesive.

Notch: Patterns indicate notches to cut. Used to line up fabric pieces when sewing. Some notches may be single while others are double.

Notions: All your sewing needs, from buttons and snaps to pressing tools. Includes interfacing, stabilizers, marking pens, needles, scissors and threads to name just a few.

One-way design: Fabrics that have a printed design that goes in one direction, requiring pattern pieces to be cut in the same direction. Use the *with nap* pattern layout.

Overcast: A finished edge that prevents raveling and can be accomplished by hand or by machine. By hand, whipstitch the raw edge. By machine, use a small zigzag or overcast stitch.

Overlock: A finished edge that prevents raveling and is usually performed by a serger that cuts the fabric at the same time.

Pattern: Templates, often made of paper, of project or garment pieces that are traced onto fabric, cut out and sewn together. A variation called a *sloper* is a custom fit pattern from which many different styles can be sewn.

Pattern weights: Objects that firmly and securely keep pattern in place while cutting. An alternative to using pins. Can be purchased, with some being bendable, or use flat washers at least 3" (8cm) in diameter for proper weight.

Picot stitch: A decorative stitch used on edgings. Picot comes from the French, meaning "small point."

Pile: The raised surface of a fabric, as with velour, velveteen and velvet.

Pins: Small pieces of metal or brass used to temporarily hold and/or mark fabrics. They can hold fabric pieces together while sewing or fitting a garment, or they can indicate where a stitching line should be.

Pin tuck: A fold or pleat that is sewn in place. Can be very narrow as in heirloom sewing, or wider for home decorative purposes.

Pinking: A method of finishing a seam. Best used on nonfraying fabrics, such as lightweight cottons. Pinking is done by trimming the seam allowances with pinking (zigzag) shears. Be sure the teeth on the sheers are sharp.

Piping: A trim consisting of a strip of folded fabric inserted into a seam, defining the edges or adding embellishment. Most often the strip is cut on the bias and folded over a cord.

Pivot: A sharp turn of the needle while sewing. To pivot, stitch to the turn or corner; stop on the upward stroke of the needle with needle down; raise presser foot; turn the fabric; lower the presser foot and continue sewing.

Placket: A slit in the garment. Usually two layers of fabric or binding are used to cover the raw edges of the slit.

Pleat: A fold(s) in the fabric that allows the fabric to be fuller in one area and fitted in another. Formed by doubling the fabric back on itself and securing in place. Pleats can be made to be seen from the right side of the garment or folded inside to be hidden.

Preshrink: Washing and drying the fabric, interlining, interfacing and stabilizer to ensure the finished item will not shrink.

Pressing: Gently lifting the iron as you move from one pressing point to another. (see *Ironing*)

Presser foot: A sewing machine attachment that holds the fabric against the feed dogs while sewing. Additional feet can be purchased to accomplish specific sewing tasks. (see *Feet*)

Pressing cloth: A cloth that is placed between your iron and fabric to prevent fabric and fiber damage to delicate fabrics, to prevent scorching, and for increased pressure when pressing darts, hems or tucks. A press cloth is 100 percent cotton (natural fiber) and absorbent. Additional moisture can be added to the cloth while pressing. A press cloth can be purchased, with newer ones made of Teflon, or create your own from cotton T-shirts, sheets and fabrics. For a heavier pressing cloth, use 100 percent wool or 100 percent cotton canvas.

Puffing: A gathered strip that is inserted and sewn between two fabric or lace pieces. Puffing is created by gathering a strip of fabric along both lengthwise sides.

Raw edge: The unfinished edge of fabric without a selvage, hem or finishing stitch.

Rickrack: Flat braid woven in a zigzag form. Available in cotton, polyester, blends, metallics, velvet and other fabrics. Used for trimming. Sizes are available as baby, medium, jumbo, giant and extra-giant. Actual sizes vary from ¼"–2½" (6.4mm–63.5mm). An wide assortment of colors are available.

Right side (fabric): The patterned side of fabric, or the side that should be seen. If the right side is not obvious, inspect and pull the fabric. Cut edges will usually roll towards the right side when stretched.

Rolled hem: A very narrow hem created with a rolled hem sewing foot. Hems can vary from 1mm–6mm wide, with the hem directly related to the size of the foot's scroll and groove on the underside.

Rotary cutter: Has a handle and a circular blade enclosed in a wheel that rotates, cutting through several layers of fabric at once. Must be used with a rotary cutting mat.

Rotary cutting mat: Used under a rotary cutter. Most are self-healing (cutting marks disappear), and have measuring grids and angles.

Ruching: Gathering a ribbon of fabric strips to form ruffles, pleats or even petals. Used for decorative detail and adding texture. A French term meaning "to gather, ruffle or pleat."

Satin stitch: Densely stitched flat stitches that resemble satin and completely cover the background fabric.

Scissors: A cutting tool with two crossed, pivoting blades. The sharpened edges glide against each other to cut. Fabric scissors are extremely sharp and blades will dull quickly if used to cut paper. Regular sewing scissors are best used for small jobs. Scissors range from about 3"–6" (8cm–15cm) in length.

Seam allowance: The area between the stitch line and the raw edge of fabric. They commonly range from ¼", ½" and ⅝" (6.4mm, 12.7mm and 15.9mm). Accurate seam allowance is crucial for professional results.

Selvage: Finished edge on either side of a piece of fabric. Firmly woven and runs parallel to the lengthwise grain.

Separating zipper: A zipper designed to separate completely from top to bottom, allowing the two sides to come entirely apart.

Shank button: A button with a hollow extended shank on the back, through which thread is sewn to attach the button to fabric. The shank button is more raised than a regular flat button. Suitable for heavy fabrics and garments, such as jackets and coats.

Shears: A type of scissor used for heavy cutting jobs. Shears generally range from 6" (15cm) and up in length. (see *Scissors*)

Shirring: Decorative sewing technique in which multiple rows of stitches, made either with regular or elastic thread, are gathered. Using elastic thread adds functionality as the garment can be gathered to fit, yet easy to remove. (see *Smocking*)

Sizing (finish): A chemical agent, such as starch, that gives stiffness to fabric. Some manufacturers apply sizing to fabric during the finishing process.

Smocking: An embroidery technique, similar to shirring, consisting of multiple rows of closely gathered stitching, usually resulting in a decorative pattern such as diamonds, herringbone or honeycomb. When sewn by machine, the decorative patterns can be done easily using built-in stitches.

Snips: Small scissors used to cut thread ends.

Spool (sewing machine): A small stand that holds the thread spool on a sewing machine. Some machines have two, one horizontal and one vertical.

Stitch length: The amount of fabric per each forward/backward stitch. A stitch length adjuster on a sewing machine adjusts the length of the stitches. The adjustment actually takes place at the feed dogs, and not the needle. When lengthening the stitch, the feed dogs lengthen the actual amount of fabric that is fed through the machine; when shortening the length, the feed dogs lessen the amount of fabric fed under the presser foot.

Stitch width: The amount of fabric per each side-to-side stitch. Machines that have zigzag capability have a stitch width adjustment. A width of 0 produces a straight stitch, and as the number increases, the width of the stitch increases.

Stiletto: A sewing tool that has a sharp point and can provide an extra "finger" when sewing. Can be used to help hold fabrics together while sewing or pressing.

Stilettos are used for making eyelet holes and are available in a variety of styles. Materials can be metal, bone and wood. Some are one "finger" while others can be two "fingers."

Straight-of-grain: Refers to the lengthwise and crosswise fibers in fabric. The true straight of grain fibers run parallel to the selvage. (see *Crosswise grain*, *Bias* and *Lengthwise grain*)

Tailor's tack: Large basted loops that temporarily keep fabric together, or transfer markings for darts.

Tape measure: Strip with linear measurements, usually in both inches and centimeters. Flexible and often made of cloth, fiber or plastic.

Tension: Refers to how tight the thread is on a sewing machine. Perfect stitches are formed when both upper and lower tension loop the stitches together properly. The upper sewing machine tension are discs that place "tension" on the thread. Bobbins also have a tension control, which is rarely adjusted.

Thimble: A small cup that is pitted on the end and worn on one finger. It is used to protect the finger that pushes the needle through the fabric while sewing by hand.

Topstitch: Stitches on the right side of the fabric, usually used as a decorative feature.

Tracing paper: (see *Carbon paper [dressmaker's]*)

Tracing wheel: A wheel on a handle used to transfer markings from a pattern onto the fabric; used in conjunction with tracing paper. Some have a serrated edge, while others are smooth.

Trim: Used as a decorative feature in garments and home decorating. Gimp, passementerie, ruffles, ribbon and braids are a few types of trim.

Tuck: A fold or a pleat in the fabric that is then sewn in place.

Universal needle: A needle that can be used on many types of fabrics for general sewing.

Velcro: A fabric hook-and-loop fastener with two layers. One side has tiny hooks that catch securely to the looped side.

Warp threads: Long threads that are stretched on a loom and secured. These become the lengthwise grain. Warp threads run parallel to the selvage. (see *Weft threads*, *Lengthwise grain*)

Walking foot: Also called an Even Feed foot. Works to keep both layers of fabric running evenly through the feed dogs. Especially useful when sewing thicker fabrics, such as with quilt layers, and other hard-to-sew fabrics, such as vinyls, leathers and "slippery" fabrics.

Weft threads: Threads that are woven back and forth perpendicular to the selvage, through the warp threads. These threads become the crosswise grain. (see *Warp threads*, *Crosswise grain*)

Welt: The seam finish used on bulky applications, such as slipcovers, pillows, or home furnishings. Welting is a cotton cord covered with a bias strip of fabric and sewn into the seam. Welting is similar to piping, but generally larger. (see *Piping*)

Wing needle: A needle with a flange on each side to create hemstitching and other decorative needlework with the sewing machine.

Woven: Woven fabric has at least two sets of yarns woven together. One set runs lengthwise and the other runs crosswise, at right angles to each other.

Wrong side: The side of the fabric that is not seen. (see *Right side*)

Zigzag stitch: A machine stitch that goes side to side. Used for finishing seams and for decoration.

Zipper: A fastener used to join two pieces of fabric. Zippers have parallel rows of plastic, metal or nylon teeth that interlock.

resources

Visit these manufacturers for more information on sewing products, notions, materials and accessories to help in all of your creative endeavors!

SEWING MACHINE COMPANIES
(for machines, feet and accessories)

Baby Lock
www.babylock.com

BERNINA USA
www.berninausa.com

Brother
www.brother-usa.com

Elna Swiss Design
www.elnausa.com/en-us

Husqvarna Viking
www.husqvarnaviking.com/us

Janome
www.janome.com

Juki Corporation
www.juki.com

Kenmore
www.kenmore.com

Pfaff USA
www.pfaffusa.com

Singer
www.singerco.com

THREAD, NEEDLES, SUPPLIES

Coats and Clark
www.coatsandclark.com

DMC
www.dmc-usa.com

Gütermann
www.guetermann.com

Isacord
http://isacordthread.com

Madeira
http://madeirausa.com

Marathon
www.marathonthread.com

Pellon
www.pellonideas.com

Robison-Anton Embroidery Thread
www.robison-anton.com

Schmetz
www.schmetz.com

Sulky
http://sulky.com

Superior Threads
www.superiorthreads.com

YLI
www.ylicorp.com

index

must-have guides for every sewer

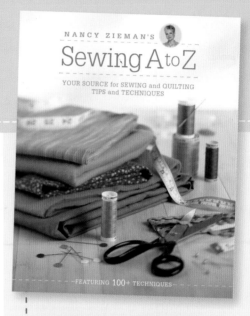

Learn to master more skills and discover great tips and tricks with the help of your favorite sewing experts.

**VISIT US AT
STORE.MARTHAPULLEN.COM**

NANCY ZIEMAN'S SEWING A TO Z

Your Source for Sewing and Quilting Tips and Techniques

by Nancy Zieman

Whether you're a novice sewer or a skilled seamstress, who better to go to for sewing answers and advice than expert Nancy Zieman? Set aside your sewing fears and let Nancy guide you step-by-step through 100+ basic to advanced sewing methods and techniques.

THE SEWING MACHINE ATTACHMENT HANDBOOK

by Charlene Philliips

If you loved *The Sewing Machine Classroom*, be sure to look for Charlene Phillips' first title, *The Sewing Machine Attachment Handbook*. This great book will teach you to identify and use 25+ of the most common sewing machine attachment feet and accessories, helping you to get the most out of your machine.

keep on sewing!

For great crafting tips, tricks and inspiration . . .

 Twitter @fwcraft

Facebook at facebook.com/fwcraft

31901051199265

KRAUSE PUBLICATIONS